COOL GEOGRAPHY

Miles of Maps,
Wild Adventures,
Fun Activities,
Facts from Around the World,
and More!

Written by Jane Glicksman

Illustrated by Ruta Daugavietis

PSS!
PRICE STERN SLOAN

To my daughter, Hallie, arbiter of cool;
my father, Jack, who put the magic in maps;
and to Eric for his valuable suggestions.
—J.G.

Library of Congress Cataloging-in-Publication Data

Glicksman, Jane.
 Cool geography : miles of maps, wild adventures, fun activities,
facts from around the world, and more! / written by Jane Glicksman :
illustrated by Ruta Daugavietis.
 p.   cm.
Includes index.
 Summary: Goes around the world, describing its maps, hemispheres,
continents, countries, and people.
 1. Geography—Juvenile literature. 2. Geography—Study and
teaching (Elementary)Activity programs—Juvenile literature.
[1. Geography.   2. Cartography—History.   3. Maps.]
I. Daugavietis, Ruta, ill.   II. Title.
G133.G55   1998   98-38551
910—dc21   CIP
                                                             AC

CONTENTS

What's So Cool About Geography?

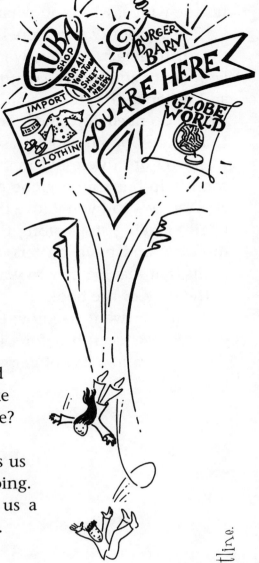

You are standing on the second floor at the mall, in front of one of those giant lighted maps. Somewhere in that maze of colors and shapes, a big red arrow says, YOU ARE HERE! But where is "here"? Is it near the food court in the blue wing or behind the music store in the purple wing? Just as you lean closer to get a better look, the ground begins to shake and shudder. With a roar, it splits apart and you fall in. As you hurtle down, you realize you aren't in an elevator. You start to worry. Will you come to rest at the bottom of the earth? Or will you pop out the other side and keep flying right on out into space? Where is the other side of the earth, exactly? And would you know anyone there? Do they like kids with backpacks? What's the dress code? Yikes!

Geography to the rescue! Geography helps us figure out where we are and where we are going. Like the map at the mall, geography gives us a directory—a really big directory—of the earth.

In 1774, Captain James Cook sailed to within 12**5** miles of the Antarctic coastline.

Geography? you ask. Isn't geography only about countries and their natural resources, national flags, and flowers? Maybe you've heard that if you memorize facts such as the capital of Peru or Cleveland's most important industry, you'll know all about the world. But there's a lot more to it than that, geographically speaking.

Did you know that geography is also about earthquakes, sonar, satellites, and deep-sea robots? Geography tells us about us, because geography IS us. It's the where, why, and what of all things related to the earth, our home.

The ancient Greeks were the first people to make a science of describing the earth. In fact, the very word *geography* in Greek means "earth description" (*geo* = earth and *graphy* = written description). The Greeks observed landmarks and distances in great detail. They created handy guidebooks for travelers, which decribed foreigners and their cultures—*How to See the World on a Drachma a Day,* perhaps?— as well as navigational guides for sailors.

If you are interested in faraway places, like to unravel mysteries, and can't help but spin a globe every time you walk by one, then you'll love geography—and you'll love this book. In *Cool Geography,* you will travel the world, making stops along the way to perform amazing activities, ponder fun facts and brain busters, and more. Here and there you'll find **bolded** terms that may be new to you. You can look up these terms in the glossary at the back of the book.

So if you want to know exactly where "here" is and see geography as you've never seen it before, just bring your curiosity and problem-solving skills. (Oh, and a bag of grapefruits will come in handy!)

The coldest recorded temperature is -128.**6**°F at Vostok, Antarctica.

COOL MAPS: THE WORLD AT YOUR FINGERTIPS

Imagine for a moment you're taking a trip—a brief excursion to Grandma's house. Do you skip over the river and through the woods? Maybe. But which river? Which woods? And, unless your house nestles against a small bubbling stream, how do you find the river that leads to the woods that will take you to Grandma's? The answers lie on a piece of paper—a *map*.

Smart kids like you looking for their grandmothers are certainly not the only people in need of maps. Mountain bikers and subway riders, weatherpersons and carpoolers, sailors and supermarket owners, ten-year-olds and eighty-year-olds—just about everyone in the world uses maps.

Maps show us where we are so that we can get to where we're going. As long as you can read and understand maps, you'll never be far from where you want to be—whether it's Grandma's or the other side of the world.

Every Picture Tells a Story: Legends, Scale, and Direction

A map is a representation, but not an exact replica, of a place. If it were, how could you take it along with you on a hike? The answer is, you couldn't, even if you had a truck. Instead, a map is an exact miniature likeness of a place, which means it is drawn to *scale*. It contains marks and figures as symbols that stand for real objects. Some of these symbols are included in the *legend*, also called a key.

The United States Geological Survey has been making maps of the United States since 1879. It has produced a list of symbols for almost

The deepest hole in the world is **7** 1/2 miles deep, in Russia's Kola **Peninsula**.

BRAIN BUSTER

Look! New Mexico!

Find a street guide of your city. Look at the index at the back to locate the grid coordinates that mark your street. See how long it takes you to find your street. Can you find your address on a highway map?

anything you would want to find on a map, such as roads and highways, airports and schools (even fence lines!), as well as all sorts of natural features, such as **volcanoes**, rivers, waterfalls, and **mountains**. If you created your own map, you could come up with your own symbols for anything you wanted to show, such as snowboarding parks, bubblegum museums, or submarine sandwich shops.

Maps show scale as a **ratio**, or comparison. For example, the scale 1:63,360 means that 1 inch on the map equals 63,360 inches on the ground, or 1 mile. Maps that cover very large distances, such as world maps, may have a scale ratio of 1:40,000,000, which means that 1 inch is equal to 631 miles (or 40 million inches!). Likewise, maps of smaller areas, such as cities, may use smaller scales. At the bottom of most maps is a **bar scale**, or a line that gives you a way to measure distances. The bar scale will have segments or tick marks for units of distance. To find the distance between two places, lay a ruler over a map and measure the space between them. Now, lay your ruler over the bar scale and measure the space there. If 1 inch on the bar scale equals 200 miles, and the distance between the two places on the map is 4 inches, then the distance between the two places on your map is 800 miles.

200 miles x 4 inches = 800 miles

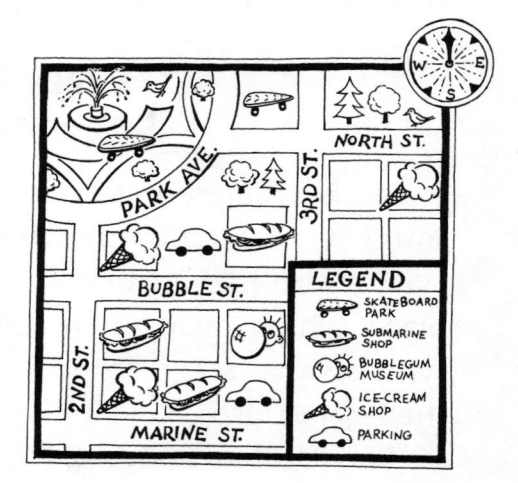

A tsunami (giant wave) can travel over **8,000** miles across the ocean in less than a day.

A feature of all maps is the ***compass rose***. It displays directional arrows for each of the cardinal directions—and that doesn't mean where the birds are going. The cardinal directions are the four main directional points on a compass: north, south, east, and west. The needle on a compass always points north. That's because the compass needle is a tiny magnet, which is attracted to the earth's north magnetic pole. Most maps place north at the top of the page, with west to the left, east to the right, and south at the bottom.

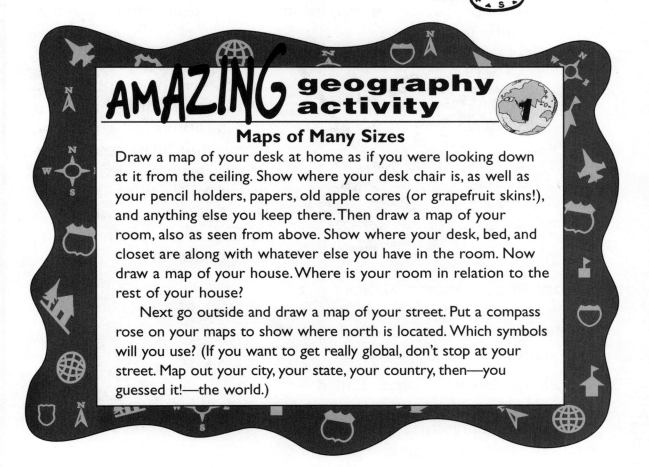

AMAZING geography activity 1

Maps of Many Sizes

Draw a map of your desk at home as if you were looking down at it from the ceiling. Show where your desk chair is, as well as your pencil holders, papers, old apple cores (or grapefruit skins!), and anything else you keep there. Then draw a map of your room, also as seen from above. Show where your desk, bed, and closet are along with whatever else you have in the room. Now draw a map of your house. Where is your room in relation to the rest of your house?

Next go outside and draw a map of your street. Put a compass rose on your maps to show where north is located. Which symbols will you use? (If you want to get really global, don't stop at your street. Map out your city, your state, your country, then—you guessed it!—the world.)

The first steel-frame skyscraper, **9** stories high, was built in Chicago, in 1885.

What if you don't have a map or a compass in front of you—can you still figure out where north, south, east, or west is? Say you head out for a short stroll in a wooded area—which turns into a long stroll because you headed south when you should have headed north. You're lost! So you reach for your compass, but oops! You didn't stick it in your pocket because, after all, you were only taking a short stroll. Now what? Look up to see where the sun is. Why? Because the sun rises in the east and sets in the west, cuing you in to your position.

The Right Map for the Job

A map can tell you so many things. Almost anything can be mapped out. Still, different maps provide different information. Here are some maps that might be familiar to you.

- **Political map:** By outlining the borders of countries and states and noting the names and locations of cities and towns, this map shows how people have divvied up the planet. So if you see a map of the United States with each state outlined, you're looking at a political map.

- **Geopolitical map:** Similar to a political map, this map shows, in addition, oceans, *lakes*, and other earth features (hence, the *geo*political).

- **Topographical map:** Called a topo map for short, this map most accurately represents the earth's natural and manmade features.

The St. Gotthard Tunnel in Switzerland is the world's longest road tunnel, at **10**.14 miles.

Contour lines show the height and steepness of *hills* and mountains and the depth of *valleys*. You can think of contour lines kind of like slices of land. The number on each line tells you the *elevation* of a place, or its height above *sea level*. Being the whiz you are, you'll notice that the closer the lines, the steeper the slope. Now, if you're a beginning hiker, you'll find topographical maps perfect for planning a trip to avoid the steepest trails or the deepest valleys.

- **Physical relief map:** Are you ready for this one? A physical relief map is like a topo map, but it really is in 3-D. It allows you to actually feel how mountainous or flat an area is. Say you wanted to open a ski resort in Australia. If you ran your finger along a physical relief map of the *continent*, you'd discover some bumpy places around the eastern and western edges, but the center would feel mostly flat. Okay, so maybe you could *build* a ski resort in western Australia. But before you start packing your boots and poles, you'd better take a look at another kind of map—a climate map.

- **Climate map:** A climate map shows long-range weather patterns of a place—whether it's usually rainy, sunny, dry, cold, or windy. Now take a look at a climate map of Australia. You'll see that most of the western part of the continent—probably colored yellow or light brown—is *desert*. (Come to think of it, maybe a ski resort in Australia is not such a good idea after all.)

- **Distribution map:** This map shows where particular groups of things are located. Let's say you wanted to find out what kinds of restaurants are located in your neighborhood. The pizza parlors might appear as red dots, ice-cream parlors as pink dots, and burger joints as green dots. If you were a chef interested in opening a restaurant far from the competition, this kind of map would be valuable indeed. Or if you lived for Burger King Whoppers, you'd simply die for a map showing all the Burger King locations in your state.

With **11** billion people, China is the most populated country in the world.

Geographer's Hall of Fame

Homer

Some people consider the poet Homer, who lived in Greece sometime before 700 B.C.E., one of the world's first geographers. Amazing, since he probably never stepped foot out of his native land! While his descriptions of the world might seem weird to us today, they reflect the thinking of most Greeks at the time. Homer wrote that the earth was a flat disc surrounded by a huge, constantly moving body of water called Oceanus. The sky rested on the earth's edge, supported by huge pillars. Homer is best known for his extremely long, non-rhyming poem *The Odyssey*, which tells about brave soldiers and their travels.

● **Road map:** You'll find one of these stuffed in almost every car's glove compartment (and usually folded wrong). This map shows how to get from point A to point B and maybe C, D, E, and Z, too. By using a road map, you can find the quickest route from Pensacola, Florida, to Washington, D.C. By looking at the shape and color of the lines on the map and at the legend, you can tell which roads are highways and which are hiking trails. If you end up on a dirt road more suitable for a tractor than a car, chances are someone didn't check the legend.

The highest waterfall in the world is Angel Falls, at 3,2**12** feet, in Venezuela.

- **Subway/bus-route map:** A subway map or a bus-route map is similar to a road map, but with even more detail. Each helps you find your way around a strange city, using the featured transportation.

- **Globe:** This spherical map is a great way to show the shape of our earth, as well as the relative size of its oceans and lands. But a globe can't show us much detail, unless it were the size of a house!

- **Atlas:** An *atlas* is a book of all kinds of maps. A world atlas might begin with a map of the entire world and then show maps of every country. It might also contain climate and distribution maps.

  Some of the coolest atlases feature a special index at the back, called a *gazetteer* (pronounced gaz-eh-TIHR). In the gazetteer you can find all sorts of weird and interesting information that doesn't show up on the maps themselves, such as where to find diners shaped like hot dogs or where the largest ball of twine is located. Gazetteers might also tell you how a certain city got its name.

Far-Out Factoid

North is north, right? Wrong! True north is where the earth spins along its axis at the North Pole (90° north latitude). Magnetic north is that point on the Northern Hemisphere that attracts one end of your compass needle. Over millions of years, the location of earth's magnetic north has moved! As of 1993, the magnetic north pole lies west of Ellef Ringnes *Island*, in the Queen Elizabeth Islands of way-northern Canada (at about 78°27' N, 104°24' W).

- **Marine chart:** A marine chart maps out what is around and under the earth's waters. It warns sailors of dangerous reefs or wrecks lying beneath the surface and also shows the safest places in a harbor to drop anchor. Plus it points out global ocean currents to help sailors of deep-oceangoing vessels to stay on course. Serious sport fishers use marine

The lowest point in the world is the Dead Sea, in southwestern Asia, at **1,3**00 feet below sea level.

charts (along with topographical maps) to scope out areas where fish are most likely to hang out—such as around old wrecks or in coves.

- **Ocean-floor map:** Until recently, the surfaces of Venus and Mars had been mapped more completely than our own oceans. In fact, a map of the earth's seafloor was about as easy to get as a round-trip coach ticket to Pluto. But satellites have changed all that. The American satellite *Geosat* and the European satellite *ERS-1* use special instruments to take images of the ocean bottom. These microwave radar images combined with sonar images taken from aboard ships have pictured undersea volcanoes, avalanches, and mountain ranges. From such images, oceanographers at the National Oceanic and Atmospheric Administration (NOAA) have produced an amazingly detailed floor-to-ceiling global map that shows the ocean floor as if all the water had been drained away! Everyone wants to get a look at an ocean-floor map—geologists studying the earth's history, oil companies searching for rich fuel deposits, fishing fleets hunting for fertile fishing grounds, even telecommunications companies seeking prime locations for laying telephone and fiber optic cables.

FAR-OUT FACTOID

To differentiate magnetic north from true north, scientists think that birds may reset their internal compasses during rest stops along their **migration** route. That would mean they can tell the difference between the constellations in the northern and southern skies! (Talk about good observation skills.)

Where Exactly Are We?: Latitude and Longitude

More than 2,000 years ago, way before computers and satellites, ancient Greek astronomers divided the earth into sections made by imaginary lines running horizontally and vertically around the earth. Modern maps still use this network of imaginary lines, called *latitude* and *longitude*, to mark the exact spot, or *absolute location*, of every place on earth. Latitude and

The construction of the Great Wall of China began in ?**14** B.C.E.

AMAZING geography activity

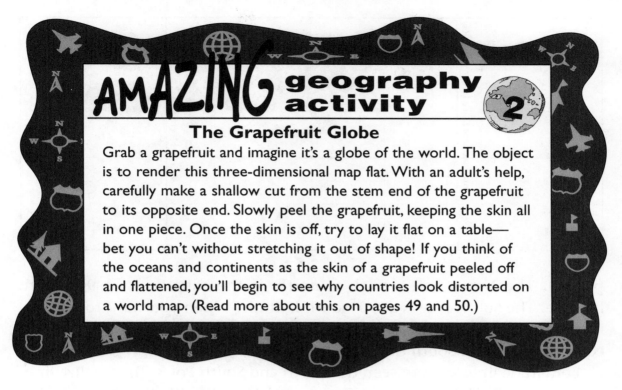

2

The Grapefruit Globe

Grab a grapefruit and imagine it's a globe of the world. The object is to render this three-dimensional map flat. With an adult's help, carefully make a shallow cut from the stem end of the grapefruit to its opposite end. Slowly peel the grapefruit, keeping the skin all in one piece. Once the skin is off, try to lay it flat on a table— bet you can't without stretching it out of shape! If you think of the oceans and continents as the skin of a grapefruit peeled off and flattened, you'll begin to see why countries look distorted on a world map. (Read more about this on pages 49 and 50.)

longitude are measured in **degrees** of arc to mark a location on the earth. What exactly is an arc? Make a *V* with your index and middle fingers. Draw an imaginary curved line to connect the tips of your fingers. There, you've drawn an arc! Degrees are divided into 60 smaller segments called minutes, and minutes are divided into 60 still smaller segments called seconds.

Latitude lines (think of the horizontal rungs on a ladder) divide the earth into equal sections north and south of the **equator**. Another word for latitude is parallel. The equator then marks 0 degrees latitude, or 0°

NORTH POLE — 90°

PRIME MERIDIAN

90° — SOUTH POLE

1° = 60 MIN.
1 MIN. = 60 SECS.

The ice in Antarctica reaches as far down as **15**,800 feet.

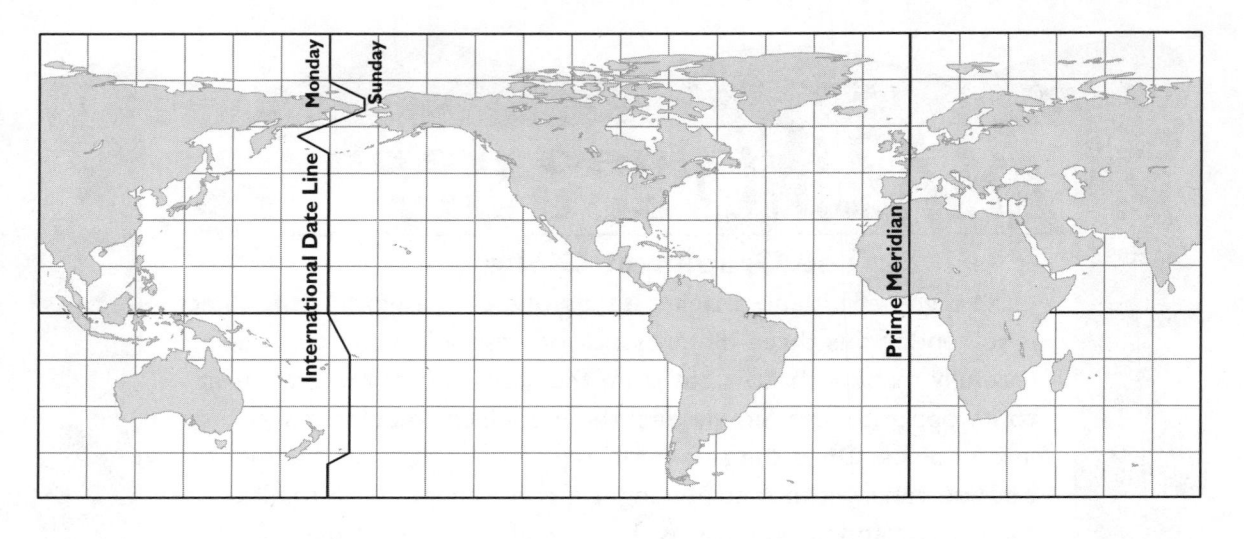

parallel. The North Pole, which is north of the equator, is at 90° north latitude. The South Pole is at 90° south latitude. When you want to find the latitude of a place, first look to see if the number has an N for north of the equator or an S for south of the equator.

Longitude lines run between the North and South Poles. To visualize lines of longitude, grab a grapefruit. Peel it and hold it with the stem-side up. Consider the lines between the sections as lines of longitude, or meridians. But unlike lines of latitude, which have the equator as the main reference point, where would we mark the first line, for 0° longitude? Since there is no perfect candidate like the equator to take this position, it took some figuring—and arguing—before line one, or the *prime meridian*, was picked to run through Greenwich, England.

Our earth takes 24 hours to complete a full revolution of 360°. It takes one hour for ¼ of a spin, or 15° of longitude (that's 360 divided by 24, for you math whizzes). Therefore, every 15° of

Look! Tennessee!

What's the time right now in the Gilbert Islands?
(Brain Buster answers on page 87.)

BRAIN BUSTER

The highest *plateau* in the world is in Tibet, about **16,000** feet above sea level.

longitude divides the earth into a segment or time zone. There are 24 time zones, one for each hour of the day. Lines of longitude show how far east or west from prime meridian a place is located. When you want to find the longitude of some place on a map, first look for the E or W following the longitudinal number. For example, 120° E means that any place along this line is 120° east of prime meridian. Look on a globe or in an atlas. Does Massachusetts lie along 71° E or 71° W? (Answer: 71°W.)

You can go east from Greenwich, England, until you reach the opposite side of the earth: 180 degrees east. If you go west 180 degrees from Greenwich, England, you'll reach the same spot! This spot is called the *international date line* (not to be confused with the lonely hearts date line). The international date line, where 180 degrees east meets 180 degrees west, separates one day from the next. Go west, gain a day. Go back east, lose a day. The clock starts

INTERNATIONAL DATE LINE

PARTY AT THE IDL (THAT'S THE INTERNATIONAL DATE LINE TO YOU!)

Here's how you can celebrate your birthday twice in one place: Buy a ticket to the Fiji Islands. On your birthday (say it's October 14), open your presents and have some pineapple cake with a few surfers. After the big day, get a good night's rest. When you wake up, take a few steps to the west, and—what do you know? You've gained a day and it's October 14 on the western side of the international date line. Pull out the cake and Pin-the-Tail-on-the-Donkey—you have another birthday to celebrate!

The 365-mile-long manmade Erie Canal began construction in the U.S. in 18**17**.

counting at 0 degree longitude, Greenwich time. See if you can figure out the following riddle:

It's noon in London and Reggie has decided to call his friend Rita, who lives at 61°13' N, 149°54' W. Why wasn't Rita thrilled to get his call?

ANSWER: She was asleep! Rita lives in Anchorage, Alaska, where it's 2 A.M.! To figure out how many hours west of England Anchorage is, divide the longitude of Anchorage (150°) by 15 and you get 10 hours. (Every 15 degrees of longitude equals one hour.) Since Alaska is west of London, count backward from noon.

Latitude and longitude lines may cover the world, but when you are looking at a smaller area on a map, they're not very useful.

BRAIN BUSTER

Look! Texas!

Can you find the place where 0° latitude meets 0° longitude? Does it intersect on land or in water?

Far-Out Factoid

The prime meridian has had many homes: In the year 200, the geographer Ptolemy put it at the Fortunate Islands (now known as the Canary Islands) off the northwest coast of Africa, where it remained for 1,000 years. After that it was a free-for-all, as every self-respecting country in the civilized world wanted the prime meridian within its borders. Rome, Copenhagen, Pisa, Paris, Philadelphia, and London, among others, hosted the prime meridian before it finally came to rest at the Greenwich Observatory near London, England in 1884.

The Grand **Canyon** in the U.S., the world's largest gorge, is **18** miles at its widest point.

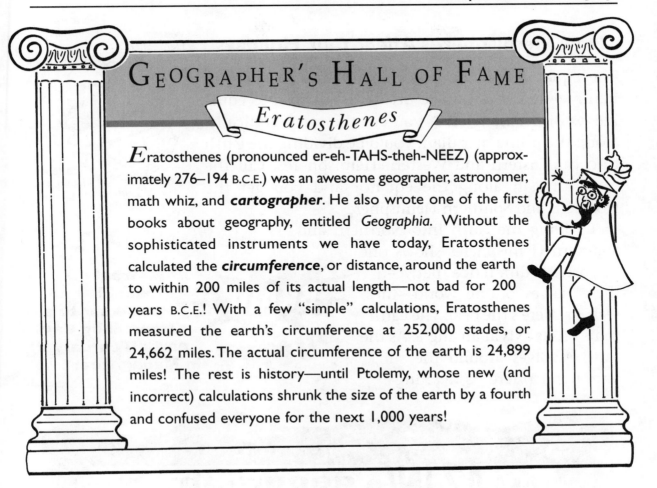

GEOGRAPHER'S HALL OF FAME

Eratosthenes

*E*ratosthenes (pronounced er-eh-TAHS-theh-NEEZ) (approximately 276–194 B.C.E.) was an awesome geographer, astronomer, math whiz, and **cartographer**. He also wrote one of the first books about geography, entitled *Geographia*. Without the sophisticated instruments we have today, Eratosthenes calculated the **circumference**, or distance, around the earth to within 200 miles of its actual length—not bad for 200 years B.C.E.! With a few "simple" calculations, Eratosthenes measured the earth's circumference at 252,000 stades, or 24,662 miles. The actual circumference of the earth is 24,899 miles! The rest is history—until Ptolemy, whose new (and incorrect) calculations shrunk the size of the earth by a fourth and confused everyone for the next 1,000 years!

The places you're looking for will probably fall through the cracks, or to be geographically correct, slip between the degree lines.

If you look at a street map, instead of longitude and latitude lines, you'll see letters running along the top and bottom margins and numbers along the right and left margins. These letters and numbers form a **grid**. Grid lines are drawn on a map to help locate places. For example, if you're looking for Hibiscus Drive in Highlands Ranch, Colorado, and the index says it's at D3, find the square on the map where the D and 3 lines cross. The grids on larger maps, such as country or world maps, often correspond to the geographic grid of latitude and longitude.

One of the highest active volcanoes is Cotopaxi, Ecuador, at **19**,347 feet.

How Hemispheres Affect Your Holidays

The equator and the prime meridian also come in handy when you want to divide the earth into equal halves or *hemispheres*. If you cut the earth vertically, along the prime meridian, you'd be dividing the earth into the Eastern and Western Hemispheres. Cut the earth in half along the equator and you get the Northern and Southern Hemispheres.

Dividing the earth into Northern and Southern Hemispheres shows one important difference between these halves of the world—the seasons. Here's the deal: The earth spins on its axis at an angle. As the earth revolves around the sun, one hemisphere is leaning

Western Hemisphere

Northern Hemisphere

Eastern Hemisphere

Southern Hemisphere

Look! Virginia!

BRAIN BUSTER

What would you wear to a Groundhog Day party (February 2) in Madagascar?

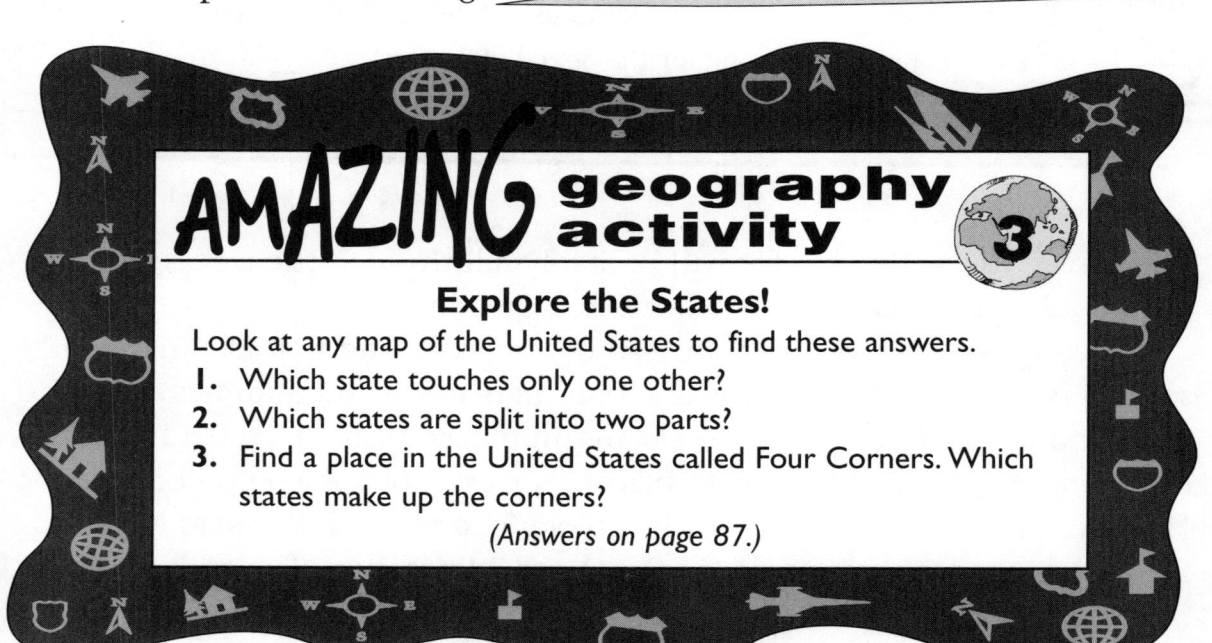

AMAZING geography activity 3

Explore the States!

Look at any map of the United States to find these answers.

1. Which state touches only one other?
2. Which states are split into two parts?
3. Find a place in the United States called Four Corners. Which states make up the corners?

(Answers on page 87.)

The windiest place is Commonwealth Bay in Antarctica, where wind speeds of over **20**0 miles per hour were clocked.

slightly toward the sun, which is more directly overhead, giving that area more light and heat. At the same time, the opposite hemisphere is leaning away, which means colder weather. Brrr. But wait! As the earth completes its orbit, the opposite hemisphere leans toward the sun. So, while many living in the Northern Hemisphere celebrate January 1 with galoshes and gloves, Australians, South Americans, and other Southern Hemisphere inhabitants bring in the New Year wearing sunscreen and swimsuits.

Way-Out Web Sites

Here are some places you can go for further exploration and information—as long as you have permission from your parents and access to a computer and the Internet:

- The United States Geological Survey (USGS) site will give you links to national and international maps and geographical information. It has cool games, too:

    http://www.usgs.gov/

- Visiting a new city? If you absolutely need to know where to find the best root beer floats, check out Citynet for info about every major city in the United States. You'll also find info about movie theaters, restaurants, amusement parks, hotels, and more:

    http://www.city.net

- Get the weather anywhere, any place from the Weathernet home page at:

    http://www.weathernet.com

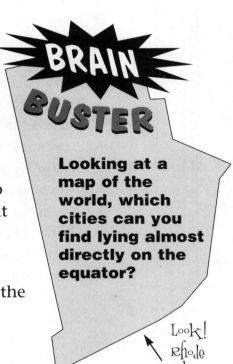

BRAIN BUSTER

Looking at a map of the world, which cities can you find lying almost directly on the equator?

Look! Rhode Island!

Rhode Island is the smallest U.S. state at 1,212 square miles.

GEOGRAPHER'S HALL OF FAME

Thales

*T*hales (625–547 B.C.E.) founded a school for the study of geography and philosophy. He traveled widely and wrote detailed descriptions of the earth and its place in the heavens as he saw it. He was one of the first to divide the earth into climate **regions**, which he called climata. Thales's amazingly accurate climata include:

- ⊕ the Arctic (what geographers now call the **polar region**)
- ⊕ the summer tropical (the **temperate** region north of the equator, having cool winters and warm summers)
- ⊕ the equatorial (where it's hot all the time)
- ⊕ the winter tropical (the temperate region south of the equator, having warm winters and cool summers)
- ⊕ the Antarctic (the southern polar region).

The big mystery still nagging people today is how Thales knew about the winter tropical area and the Antarctic region. In his day, no Greek had ever been south of the equator—or if they had, they never lived to write about it!

Thales also created a system for measuring distances, called the stade, which is very much like the system of miles and kilometers used today.

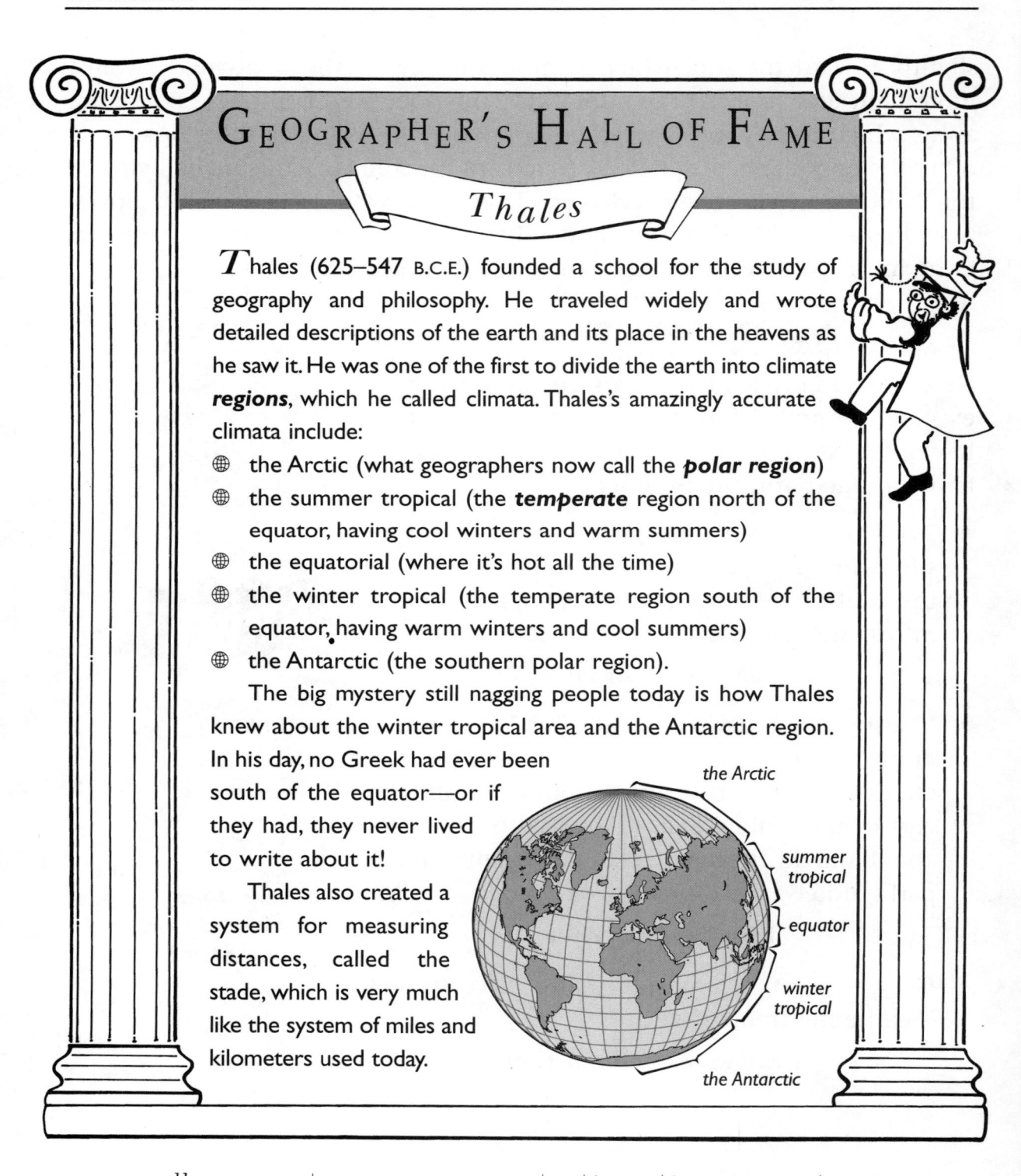

the Arctic

summer tropical

equator

winter tropical

the Antarctic

Magellan's expedition circumnavigated the earth from 1519 to 15**22**.

COOL EXPLORERS: THEY CAME, THEY SAW, THEY DISCOVERED THE WORLD

Just imagine standing on an empty beach, knowing you were the first person from your country to view this spectacular sight. Nobody else has waded in its waters, built castles in its sands, or watched the sun set from this spot. Like past explorers, you could name the land after yourself, then rush back home to spread word of your discovery. Or maybe this would mark just the beginning of exploration of yet more lands.

As you will see, some of the world's earliest explorers had all sorts of reasons for leaving their homelands: the possibility of riches and fame, a fascination with the unknown, even escape from the law. Regardless of what motivated them, these explorers helped to shape our world.

The First Wave of Cool Explorers

Hannu: The Pharaohs ruling Egypt nearly 5,000 years ago had very expensive tastes. Since no gourmet markets or shopping malls were nearby, somebody had to make the shopping trips for such items as ebony (and ivory) and panther skins. In 2,400 B.C.E. Hannu took the job and set sail for the legendary land of Punt. While there were other explorers during this time, Hannu

*North America is made up of **23** countries.*

wanted to make sure his exploits would go down in history. He therefore had the story of his successful expedition to Punt carved on a stone tablet. Although historians aren't sure where Punt was located, some think it was near the country of Somalia, north of the equator. Nobody has even been able to figure out what the name *Punt* means (or if this place has anything to do with football)!

The Phoenicians: As the first ancient seafaring people to sail out of sight of land, the Phoenicians really rocked. They ruled the seas and kept it that way by spreading rather gruesome tales to keep others from crowding their trade routes.

According to the Greek historian and geographer Herodotus, in 600 B.C.E. Egypt's King Necho sent an expedition of Phoenician sailors to explore the coastline of Africa. The journey began at the Red Sea and went on through what was then called the Southern Ocean (today's Indian Ocean). The sailors then eventually passed through what was then known as the Pillars of Hercules at the western end of the Mediterranean Sea and back to Egypt. The Pillars of Hercules are a narrow body of water—a *strait*—sheltered on both sides by towering cliffs. This tremendous 13,000-mile journey took about three years to complete. At its end, the Phoenicians had

What are the Pillars of Hercules called today?

Look! North Carolina!

circumnavigated the continent of Africa, a voyage no one dared repeat until the Portuguese explorer Vasco da Gama tried, and succeeded, 2,000 years later.

Alexander the Great: During his lifetime, Alexander the Great (356–323 B.C.E.) traveled overland more than 20,000 miles from Greece east through Persia, Afghanistan, Turkey, and India. (If that mileage were spread out over his entire lifetime, Alex would have traveled 600 miles every year of his life, from birth to death.) Some of his armies sailed the Indian Ocean north

The Great Barrier Reef in Australia is the world's largest living thing, a coral colony over 1,240 miles long.

through the Persian *Gulf*, up the Euphrates River, and into the Mediterranean Sea, opening a new sea route to the East.

One reason Alexander the Great was so great was that he thought like a true geographer. On his expeditions, he brought along *bematists* (these were people who measured distances by walking), naturalists, historians, and philosophers, and kept records of all their discoveries. By counting the steps of his marching soldiers, Alexander mapped his way from India and back.

Pytheas: Pytheas, who lived in the Greek colony of Massilia (now Marseilles, France), traveled in different circles from Alexander the Great. While Alex and his crew headed east, Pytheas went north, looking for a fabulous—and rich—place called the Tin Islands, above what the Greeks called Europa (today's Europe). Pytheas and his men sailed north into the Atlantic Ocean and across the English Channel. They bumped into England and Ireland and later docked at a mysterious land called Thule, north of Scotland. Pytheas's descriptions of the voyage were so weird that some people thought he had gone mad. According to Pytheas's journal, Thule, which may have been Iceland or the Faeroe Islands, was a six-day sail to the north in the middle of what people called the Frozen Ocean. "Here, there is neither sea nor air but a mixture like sea-lung in which the earth and air are suspended; the sea-lung binds everything together." This "sea-lung" may have been fog and ice—something the warm-weather Greeks had never seen. Pytheas also reported that the sun shone for 24 hours a day during the summer—hard at that time for most people to the south to believe!

Chang Ch'ien: In 120 B.C.E., the Chinese Emperor ordered the explorer Chang Ch'ien into "the unknown" to seek out a tribe called the Yue-Chi. The emperor believed the Yue-Chi could help China fight off their enemies, the Huns, a fierce tribe of warriors. (You may have heard of their charming leader, Attila.) Almost immediately, however, Chang Ch'ien was captured by the Huns and imprisoned. But life as a captive was not as harsh as you might imagine. Even though he remained a prisoner for over 10 years, Chang Ch'ien married, had a family, and traveled in style with the Huns on their raids. Still,

Over **25** percent of the Netherlands lies below sea level.

the loyal Chang Ch'ien never forgot his orders from the emperor. When he managed to escape from the Huns, he made his way north over the Gobi Desert to complete his mission. He finally tracked down the Yue-Chi in Bactria (now Afghanistan). Unfortunately, the Yue-Chi had their own problems and weren't interested in helping the Chinese emperor fight any battles. It took Chang Ch'ien 10 years to get no help!

The trip was not a total loss, however, for Chang Ch'ien learned about many rich countries beyond China's border. He established trading relationships with India and Persia and presented the emperor with horses when he returned—13 years after the day he left! His expeditions not only opened China's world, they also linked the country to the West by way of the Silk Road, pictured above.

Cheng Ho: After Chang Ch'ien's exploits, there were no major Chinese explorations until hundreds of years later. In 1405, the Chinese sent out another expedition,

Far-Out Factoid

No, the Silk Road, also called the Silk Route, was not made of silk. (The term *Silk Route* was not even coined until the nineteenth century.) But at 5,600 miles, it was the greatest long-distance trade route ever, bringing porcelain, spices, gold, and, yes, silk to the Western world. It linked China, the Middle East, and later the countries of Europe.

Before the Berlin Wall was knocked down in 1989, it ran **26**.5 miles long.

THE POLYNESIANS— THE ORIGINAL ISLAND HOPPERS

The Polynesians sailed in huge double-hulled canoes that could carry hundreds of people, as well as animals and plants, for long voyages. It is thought they began their migration from Melanesia. They hopped from island to island among the thousands of Pacific Islands, gradually inhabiting many of them. They reached the Hawaiian Islands, more than 1,200 miles from any other island, around the year 300—and were possibly the first settlers there. Did they plan to travel that far or did they get blown off course by storms? No one knows for sure.

but this time on a larger scale. Cheng Ho's fleet of more than 300 ships held 27,500 men! The largest of these ships had nine masts and was more than 400 feet long—longer than a football field. In comparison, Christopher Columbus's three ships each measured only about 90 feet long.

Over the course of nearly 30 years, Cheng Ho explored Japan, Borneo, India, and East Africa in journeys as far west as the Persian Gulf and the Red Sea.

The Age of Discovery

Exploration fever in Europe reached its peak in the fifteenth century. The Portuguese prince Henry the Navigator spent his life perfecting the art of navigation so that the European nations, especially Portugal, would increase in power and wealth by claiming new lands. In the early 1440s, Henry got things rolling by launching seagoing expeditions to the west coast of Africa. When his sailors brought back treasure from their trips, a waterlogged stampede to the East began that lasted more than 200 years.

On August **27**, 1883, Krakatoa, in Indonesia, erupted and was heard 2,200 miles away.

Craving gold, spices, and free labor (slaves stolen from their homelands), Portuguese, Spanish, and English kings quickly sent out expeditions. "Fill our banks and find more lands to enrich our empires!" they ordered. However, the eager kings were probably not very kind when it came to the lives of the seamen. Many sailors never returned home from the long and dangerous expeditions. But those who did filled in the blanks on the world map with many surprises.

The Portuguese

The Portuguese were aggressive in their early explorations. In 1486, Portuguese navigator Bartholomeu Dias discovered the **Cape** of Storms (now the Cape of

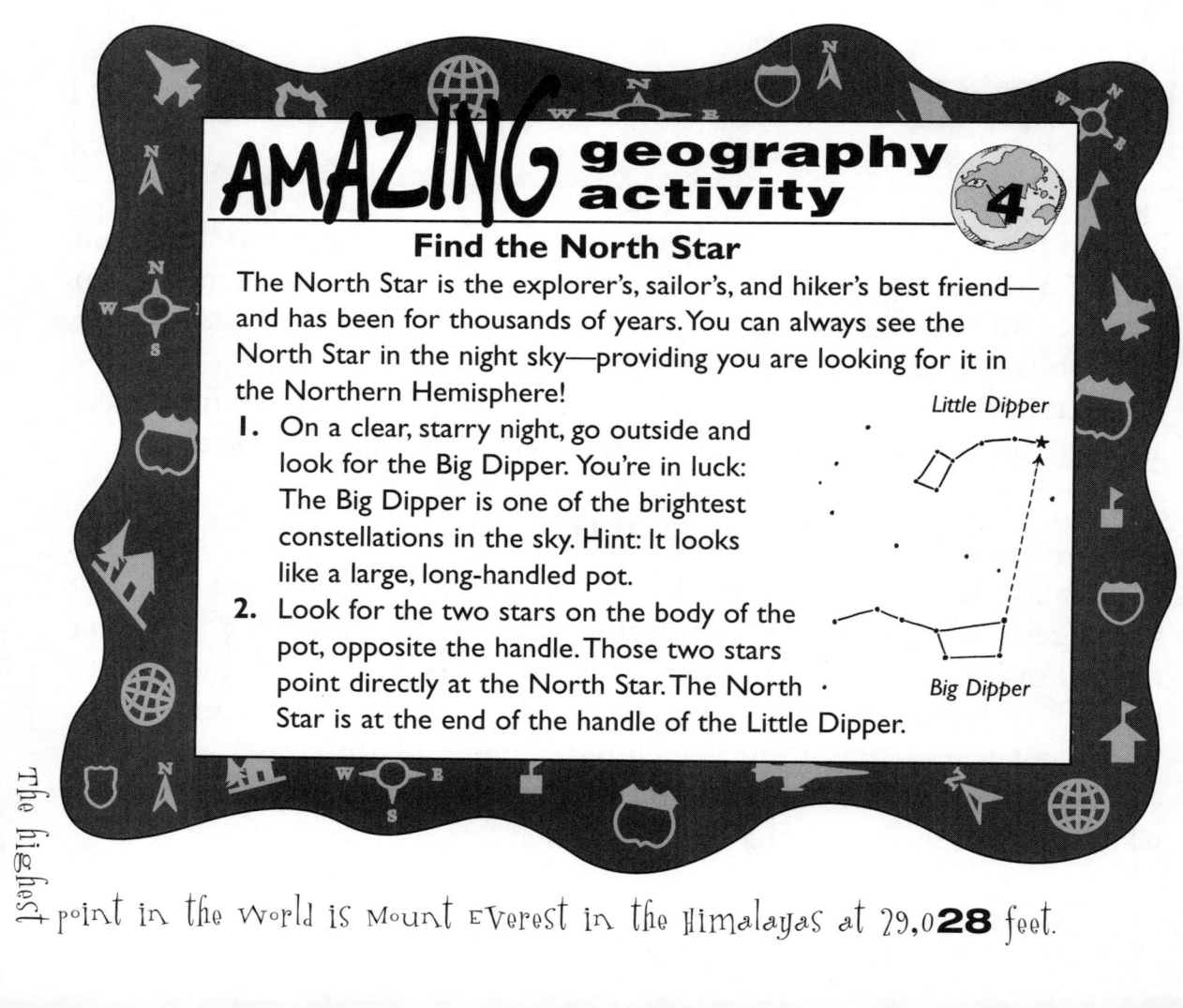

AMAZING geography activity 4

Find the North Star

The North Star is the explorer's, sailor's, and hiker's best friend—and has been for thousands of years. You can always see the North Star in the night sky—providing you are looking for it in the Northern Hemisphere!

1. On a clear, starry night, go outside and look for the Big Dipper. You're in luck: The Big Dipper is one of the brightest constellations in the sky. Hint: It looks like a large, long-handled pot.

2. Look for the two stars on the body of the pot, opposite the handle. Those two stars point directly at the North Star. The North Star is at the end of the handle of the Little Dipper.

Little Dipper

Big Dipper

Good Hope) while sailing the western coast of Africa. In 1497, Vasco da Gama, another Portuguese navigator, sailed around the Cape and up Africa's eastern coast on his way to India. The Portuguese were convinced there was a sea route east of India to Asia's Spice Islands (now a part of Indonesia). They were right.

Can you imagine traveling across the ocean in search of cinnamon? Or nutmeg? But that's just what many European explorers did. They set sail for the Spice Islands and not just because they were fond of cinnamon on their toast. Spices were considered very valuable and meant vast wealth for whoever found and possessed them.

Christopher Columbus: The New Continent Got in the Way

Some sailors were stubbornly convinced it would be quicker to head west to get to the Far East! Using the maps of the ancient geographer Ptolemy, Christopher Columbus persuaded King Ferdinand and Queen Isabella of Spain to finance his journey. Big mistake.

If Christopher Columbus had consulted Eratosthenes's calculations of the earth instead of Ptolemy's, he might have taken a few more supplies for his trip across the Atlantic. Ptolemy's map shrunk the earth to 18,000 miles around, rather than the 24,662 Eratosthenes had figured. In addition, Ptolemy's map expanded the area of Asia, shrinking the size of the Atlantic Ocean (and completely leaving out North and South America!).

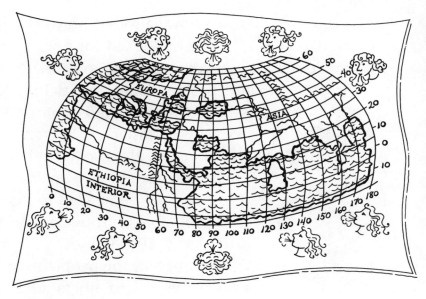

When Columbus finally reached land (the seafaring term is "made landfall") in the Bahamas, the golden buildings of the Indies

The largest **cave** is the Sarawak Chamber in Borneo and is 2,**29**7 feet long.

were nowhere to be seen. But this didn't stop Columbus. He was positive Asia lay just beyond those islands, and he made three more trips across the Atlantic to prove it. His second trip got him to the island of Cuba, where again there were no fabulous kingdoms, no gold, no spices. When his crew began to doubt his theories, Columbus demanded they all take an oath that Cuba was the southeastern coast of Asia.

On his third trip, Columbus landed at Trinidad and later hit the coast of South America, near Venezuela. Finding a huge river emptying into the Atlantic, Columbus figured he was finally at a real live continent. Referring to biblical maps which were popular at the time, Columbus decided he'd reached Paradise, the land of the Garden of Eden.

Columbus's fourth voyage took him to Honduras in Central America, where he looked for a waterway to the other side. But he never found one and finally returned to

Spain. Besides fame and riches, King Ferdinand and Queen Isabella of Spain had promised Columbus the position of viceroy (similar to governor) over all the lands he discovered. He also would have been appointed a royal admiral, gotten his own coat of arms, and been knighted, to boot. All he needed to do was find gold or something else valuable to bring back to Spain. Equally important to the King and Queen was that Columbus convert to Christianity all the people he met on his journey. When he found no gold and no fabulous hordes of spices or other

Christopher Columbus

BRAIN BUSTER

Look! Nevada!

When Columbus sailed westward from the Canary Islands, he figured that if he sailed along the 29th parallel, he'd bump into Japan. But along the way, Columbus fell off course and reached the Bahama Islands. Where would he have landed if he had stayed on course?

The largest active geyser in the world is Steamboat in Yellowstone National Park, which sends water more than **300** feet into the air.

treasures, Columbus brought converted Christianized slaves to Spain. In doing so, he paved the way for 400 years of the slave trade.

Ferdinand Magellan's Secret Strait

Like Columbus, Portuguese captain Ferdinand Magellan was sure the Spice Islands in the East could be reached by sailing west. What Magellan needed, though, was a map. Competition for trade routes was so fierce that accurate maps were hard to come by. Keeping his eyes and ears open for leads, Magellan heard of a secret from a mapmaker and astronomer named Ruy Faleiro (pronounced fehl-YEHR-oh). The secret? All Magellan had to do to reach the Spice Islands was to sail west from Europe, down the new continent, South America, and across a strait to Asia.

Ferdinand Magellan

In 1520, Magellan and his crew of 250 did find this strait, and they beat their way through a maze of channels at the tip of South America to a whole new ocean, which Magellan called the Pacific (yes, that's the ocean bordering Washington, Oregon, and California). It took 38 days to make the crossing. Unfortunately, the famed Spice Islands were not a hop, skip, and a jump away. In fact, it took 14 weeks of sailing the Pacific before they found land: the island of Guam. After a brief rest there, Magellan and his crew landed in the Philippines. Tragically, Magellan was killed there in a local war. The crew again set sail,

Far-Out Factoid

While waiting out bad weather before starting through the strait and around Cape Horn in the southernmost part of South America, today known as the Strait of Magellan, Magellan made contact with the native population. He called the people Patagonians, which means "big-footed people" in Spanish. They really didn't have such big feet, only large shoes made of animal skin, which were insulated with straw.

The highest airport in the world is at Lhasa, Tibet, 14,**31**5 feet above sea level.

eventually reaching lands the Portuguese had settled in previous expeditions. The last remaining ship—and the first ship to circle the globe—sailed the Indian Ocean, rounded the Cape of Good Hope of Africa, and finally arrived at Seville, Spain. After three years at sea, only 17 sailors remained out of the 200-plus crew.

Exploring the Ocean Blue

When you think about the immensity of the oceans (three-fourths of the earth's surface), it's hard to believe anyone would venture out to sea without the tools we have today—satellite, radar, radio, and sonar. But they did.

As early as the twelfth century, Mediterranean sailors used a compass, probably invented by the Chinese in 1100. With early navigation tools, such as the cross-staff, *astrolabe*, and quadrant, the navigator could observe the position of the stars and planets and calculate the ship's latitude. But there was no accurate way to figure out a ship's longitude. (Remember: Greenwich, England, became the permanent home for the prime meridian in 1884.) With no landmarks or signs, it was impossible to know exactly where one was or how far one had traveled in an east/west direction over the ocean. Because of this lack of information, there were many tragedies at sea. If a navigator misjudged the amount of time a journey would take or if a ship were blown off course, sailors starved for lack of food. Other times boats were torn apart by reefs or rocks because the navigator miscalculated the ship's position at sea.

Thunder occurs **322** days a year at Bogor in Java, Indonesia.

Well, guess what? The biggest techno quest of the early eighteenth century was finding a way to fix accurate longitude. Finally, a contest was offered to come up with a solution. A Board of Longitude, made up of scientists, astronomers, and political officials, was formed to judge the contestants and dole out the prize money. The race was on!

Astronomers proposed that navigators calculate a ship's position by keeping a log of the phases of Jupiter's moons. The only problem was that a navigator would have to perform hours of mathematical calculations, and the night sky had to be clear enough for an observer to actually see Jupiter. A few believed the key was in a clock. Here's why: There are 24 hours in a day—the time it takes the earth to make one complete turn. So one hour

REWARD

A KING'S RANSOM FOR THE LONGITUDE

A PRIZE OF £20,000* FOR PRACTICABLE AND USEFUL MEANS OF DETERMINING LONGITUDE TO AN ACCURACY OF HALF A DEGREE OF A GREAT CIRCLE.

By the Longitude Act, issued by the reign of Queen Anne on July 8, 1714

* EQUALS MORE THAN A MILLION DOLLARS TODAY!

A WEIRD SOLUTION TO LONGITUDE

Long before the Board of Longitude was formed, the great astronomer and scientist Galileo (1564–1642) invented a special navigation helmet, called the celatone, to help navigators find Jupiter. It looked a lot like a gas mask with a telescope attached to one of the eyeholes. The other eyehole was empty. Looking through the empty eyehole, the wearer could locate the planet Jupiter in the sky. By then peering through the telescope eyehole, the observer could see the moons of Jupiter. The problem? Galileo admitted that the pounding of his heart made the telescope shake so violently that absolutely nothing could be seen!

represents ¼₄ of a turn. And ¼₄ of a turn can also be represented by 15° of longitude. (360° equals a full turn, so 15° equals ¼₄ turn.) Thus degrees of longitude can be translated into a period of time by marking off 24 time meridians at specific lines of longitude, starting at 0° longitude (Greenwich, England). Every time meridian is an hour apart in time and 15° apart in location. Each hour's time difference between the ship and the starting point marks a progress of 15° longitude east or west. Unfortunately, no one had been able to produce a clock that kept accurate time on the wet and rolling decks of a ship.

But one stubborn man named John Harrison would not let a few drenching waves stop him. He quietly worked at building the perfect timekeeper, and in 1735, the first marine clock, or **chronometer**, was completed. However, it took several years for the Board of Longitude to agree that John Harrison's chronometer was indeed an accurate way to find longitude. Even then, he never received the full amount of the prize money. What a ripoff!

AN EVEN WEIRDER SOLUTION TO LONGITUDE

In the 1730s, the Wounded Dog Theory was introduced to solve the problem of keeping accurate time aboard ship. A miracle powder called the Powder of Sympathy was said to heal wounds at a distance. All you had to do was apply it to something owned and worn by the ailing person, like a bandage. However, when applied, the powder stung the flesh. (We told you this was weird!) To use the Powder of Sympathy for the longitude problem, all one had to have was a wounded dog and an accurate clock on board ship. At noon every day, a person on land would sprinkle the Powder of Sympathy on an ailing dog's bandage, and—voilà!—the dog on the ship would yelp in reaction. If the captain's watch said 2 P.M. when the dog barked, it would be two hours past London time. Problem solved.

For the captain, perhaps, but not for the dog!

Kilimanjaro in Tanzania is the highest mountain in Africa at 19,**34**0 feet.

AMAZING geography activity 5

Finding Your Latitude from the North Star

To do this activity, you will need: pencil, 5-by-5-inch poster board, protractor, scissors, hole punch, string, paper clip, small weight (a nail, washer, sinker), plastic drinking straw, and tape.

1. On the poster board, draw a vertical line down the left side and a horizontal line along the top, about ½ inch from the edges. Line the straight edge of the protractor against the left line on the poster board, as shown.

2. Mark off and label the degrees in units of 5: 0, 5, 10, 15, 20, and so on.

3. Place the protractor on the poster board. Then with your scissors, trim the poster board around the curved part of your protractor.

4. Using the hole punch, punch a small hole at the corner, where the lines cross. Thread one end of the string through the hole.

5. Tie that end to the paper clip to keep the string from slipping through. Tie the other end of the string to the small weight.

6. Tape the plastic drinking straw to the top edge of the poster board, along the 90° mark.

7. At night, look for the North Star (turn to Amazing Geography Activity #4 on page 28 for help). Now hold your sighting tool as shown and look through the straw. When you sight the North Star, the string will mark the degree of latitude of your location.

On average, it rains **35**0 days in a year at Mount Wai-'ale-'ale in Hawaii.

The Northwest Passage

While the southern Europeans were going West to find the East, the English, as well as the French and Dutch, were certain the answer lay to the north. Word of this shortcut came from Heaven itself, at least according to an English geographer named Roger Barlow, who wrote in 1540 that "the shortest route, the northern, has been reserved by Divine Providence for England."

Between the years 1534 and 1650, English, along with French and Dutch, sailors searched in vain for the Northwest Passage in what is now northern Canada and the Arctic Circle. Some, like Martin Frobisher, Henry Hudson, and William Baffin, found their way blocked by either ice or land. Henry Hudson sailed through what's now called the Hudson Strait and on into Hudson Bay—but all he got for his trouble was a mutiny! It wasn't until hundreds of years later in 1903 that the Norwegian explorer Roald Amundsen actually managed to sail through northern Canada. Amundsen and his crew of seven made it to Herschel Island in the Yukon in 1906.

Accidental Discoveries

We don't know exactly when Scandinavian warriors called Vikings began roaming the western seas. The first tales of their discoveries circulated around the early ninth century. We do know that they made contact with the New World half a millennium before Columbus. And we also know they had cool ships called longboats and knorrs—and a lot of nerve. They certainly didn't let a few storms at sea slow them down. But three such storms did push them much farther from  home than they had planned—resulting in the discovery of significant lands in the North Atlantic, such as Iceland and Greenland.

The deepest **ocean trench** (canyon) is Marianas Trench, at **36**,198 feet deep.

Accident #1: Heading for the Faeroe Islands, a Viking outpost a few hundred miles north of what is now Scotland, a warrior named Naddod was blown seriously off course in a gale sometime in the year 860. When the storms cleared, Naddod saw—smoke! The land ahead was covered with volcanoes and *glaciers*. This didn't much interest Naddod, who turned around and sailed on to the Faeroes. But his reports intrigued others, and by 874 this island became a Norse colony. It was named Iceland.

Accident #2: Sometime between 900 and 930 in a powerful storm, Gunnbjorn Ulfsson skidded west of Iceland into an island of ice and rock. By 982, the land he called Gunnbjorn's Skerry was settled by a man named Erik the Red, an outlaw in need of new territory. (*Skerry* is the Norse word for "island.") Erik renamed the land Greenland in an apparently successful attempt to lure colonists, as it soon became another Norse colony.

Accident #3: This third great unintentional discovery was made by Bjarni Herjolfsson, who sighted North America after being lost in the fog around 985. Finding the continent unappealing, however, he sailed back to the land he preferred—Greenland!

After hearing Herjolfsson's story, Leif Eriksson, son of Erik the Red, sailed out to take a closer look at North America. Around the year 1000, Eriksson became the first European to walk on North American ground. He called the

Far-Out Factoid

Without the use of the fancy gizmos available to travelers today, Viking sailors supposedly used their feathered friends to help them navigate. If a bird released from a ship flew off toward the direction they had sailed from and didn't return, the sailors assumed their boats were not far from the land they'd just left. But if the bird returned, that meant the ship was far from land. Finally, after a few days or weeks, if a bird was released again and didn't return, that meant new land was nearby.

The deepest part of the ocean is **37,000** feet, a place where no one has been.

place Vinland, or fruitful land. Today this is Newfoundland. The Vikings spent a few years trying to settle the new land but were finally driven off by the locals, most likely Inuit or forest-dwelling Native Americans. But the next time Europeans landed on North American shores, they were there to stay.

North Pole Firsts by Land, Sea, and Air

By the early twentieth century, the North Pole was one of the last surface areas on earth yet to be fully explored. Adventurers, scientists, and record

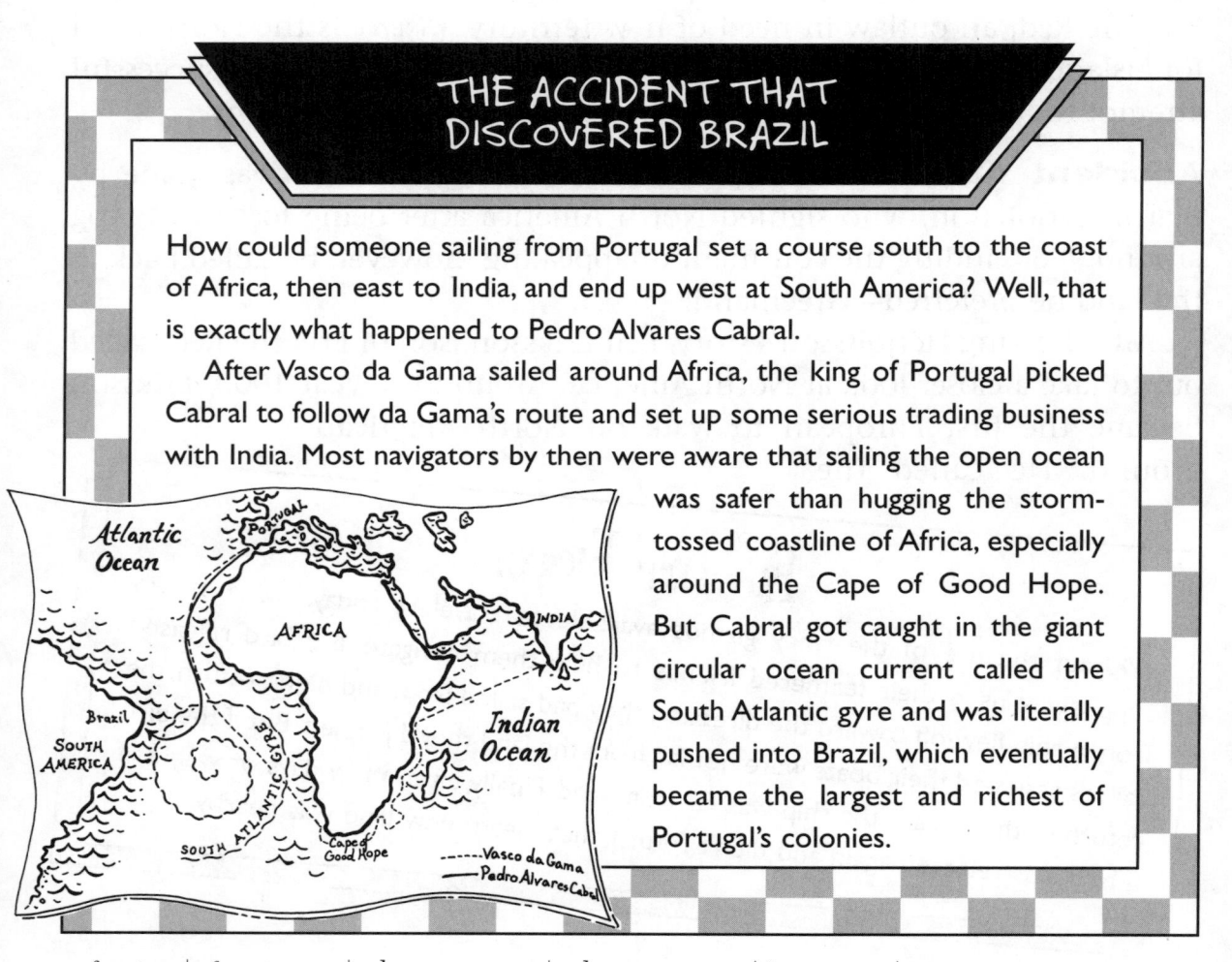

THE ACCIDENT THAT DISCOVERED BRAZIL

How could someone sailing from Portugal set a course south to the coast of Africa, then east to India, and end up west at South America? Well, that is exactly what happened to Pedro Alvares Cabral.

After Vasco da Gama sailed around Africa, the king of Portugal picked Cabral to follow da Gama's route and set up some serious trading business with India. Most navigators by then were aware that sailing the open ocean was safer than hugging the storm-tossed coastline of Africa, especially around the Cape of Good Hope. But Cabral got caught in the giant circular ocean current called the South Atlantic gyre and was literally pushed into Brazil, which eventually became the largest and richest of Portugal's colonies.

The first humans to live in Australia arrived there about **38,000** years ago.

breakers from around the world raced to be the first to plant their flag on this far-out edge of the planet.

In 1909 an American explorer, Robert Peary, proved there was no new continent under the ice of the North Pole. Arriving by sled to within five miles of the pole, Peary made soundings under the ice as deep as 10,000 feet without ever finding land. Like Peary, most explorers made their trips to the frozen north by dogsled, ice-breaking boat, or later, by plane. Some had other ideas. In 1968 Ralph Plaisted reached the actual North Pole by snowmobile!

The first person to claim to reach the pole by air was Richard E. Byrd. With Floyd Bennett as pilot, he set out from Spitsbergen, Norway, on May 9, 1926. The first surface ship to reach the pole was the Soviet nuclear icebreaker *Arktika* in 1977. In 1958 the U.S. nuclear submarine *Nautilus* reached the pole under the ice cap.

Far-Out Factoid

About 80 percent of all the world's living things make their home in the ocean. In the very deep oceans, scientists think there may be 10 million species we've never even seen!

The Deep:
The Explorers' Final Frontier

Until the late nineteenth century, deep-sea exploration was little more than a dream. After all, who could hold their breath long enough to discover anything? But curiosity drove people to invent machines that would allow them to explore the three-fourths of the world that is underwater.

The first diving bell, a small air-filled cabin, was built by an English engineer in the late 1700s. In the next century the first diving suits were used, and later, in 1943, Jacques Cousteau invented the SCUBA (Self-Contained Underwater Breathing Apparatus).

Perhaps the most dramatic deep-sea voyage was taken by Jacques Piccard and another scientist in 1960, and it was a doozy. Their submarine called *Trieste*

Germany invaded Poland in 19**39**, which began World War II.

plummeted 35,800 feet into the Marianas Trench, the world's deepest known oceanic abyss.

Since then, the tools and technology for ocean exploration have become more and more like science fiction!

The deep-sea robot *Jason,* for example, is a remote-operated vehicle (ROV) that can hang out in depths of up to 20,000 feet.

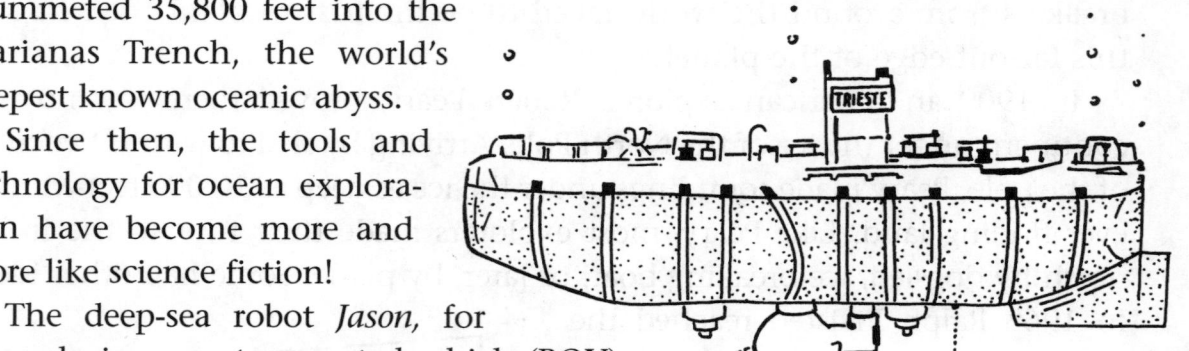

AMAZING geography activity 6

Find the latitude and longitude opposite your location.

Did anyone ever tell you that if you dug a hole deep enough, you'd end up in China? How do you really know that China is exactly opposite from where you are standing? Try this experiment and see.

1. Find your latitude and longitude on a map. An atlas will give the exact location for your city.

2. To find the opposite latitude, change your latitude to the opposite direction. For example, if you are at 40° N, change it to 40° S.

3. To find the opposite longitude, subtract your longitude from 180. Then change the direction of the difference to the direction opposite yours. For example, the longitude of Hawaii is 158° W. Subtract 158 from 180 to get 22. Then change the answer to the opposite direction. The opposite longitude is 22° E.

No rain has fallen in the Anacama Desert in northern Chile in **40**0 years.

Some of *Jason*'s first expeditions were explorations in the Atlantic Ocean of the wreck of the *Titanic*.

One of the coolest new deep-sea explorers doesn't even look like a ship. *Deep Flight I* is more like a rocket, pointed straight down to the bottom of the sea and is called a winged submersible. *Deep Flight*'s maiden voyage was completed in October of 1996. *Deep Flight II* is under construction.

More Way-Out Web Sites

Here is a real place you can go—as long as you have permission from your parents and access to a computer and the Internet:

◉ Virtual explorers have slithered along the depths of the Atlantic Ocean and crawled along the decks of the *Titanic* at the bottom of 13,000 feet of water with *Jason*, an underwater robot called an ROV (remote-operated vehicle). Follow the *Jason* Project on the World Wide Web:

http://www.jasonproject.org

Far-Out Factoid

Fish are perfectly suited for ocean life, right? Then why not build a submersible that works like a fish? Actually, someone has, and its name is *Robotuna*! A fish swims by moving its tail side to side, propelling it through the water. This idea was adapted to *Robotuna*, which has a flexible "skeleton" that enables it to "wiggle" through the water. So far, this robot fish has only made a few test dives in a laboratory tank. But it won't be long before the real fish get their scales knocked off by this new kid on the block!

An **iceberg** from Antarctica floated more than 3,418 miles north.

COOL MAPMAKING: From Clay Tablets to Computer Graphics

Maps are our windows to the world, and cartographers are the artists who make them. Over the centuries, maps have been made of nearly everywhere on, in, and above the earth: star charts; harbors, coastlines, and mountain ranges; even city maps locating telephone and electrical lines. By the early twentieth century, not much was left to be discovered on land, although there was still plenty left for cartographers to map. Today, technology is making it possible to map even those places people can't (or won't!) physically go, such as the ocean depths or the moons of Jupiter.

Old Maps, Bold Maps

Early ideas about the shape of the earth and the lands and oceans on it may seem strange to us today. But long ago, few people left their homes to go exploring, so they had to rely on the reports of those who did. And these people very often embroidered the truth or filled in the blanks with their own imaginations. The ones who drew maps lacked the technology of compass, let alone radar: They had only the sun, moon, and stars to guide them. This led to many "educated guesses" when drawing!

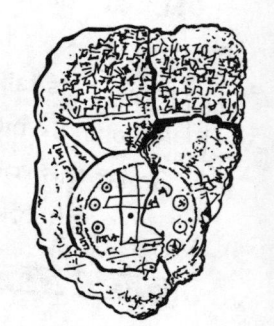

Babylonia, 4000 B.C.E.: One of the oldest maps still intact shows the ancient city of Babylonia. Produced on clay,

The Scientist Galileo died in 16**42**.

it was like a street map, showing property boundaries. If you could read the ancient writing called cuneiform, you'd be able to tell where people lived, how big their backyards were, and how much tax they paid that year!

The World, 550 B.C.E.: According to a map made by the ancient Greek mathematician Anaximander, the rectangular habitable world was surrounded by an endless ocean. The sun disappeared at night, explained Anaximander, because it was then hidden by high mountains at the northern end of the world.

Rome, third century: This Roman map is one of the earliest road maps in the world. It shows a network of mountains, bodies of water, roads, houses, and various buildings belonging to important people. A copy was found between the eleventh and twelfth centuries. It was probably copied from an earlier map used for war raids.

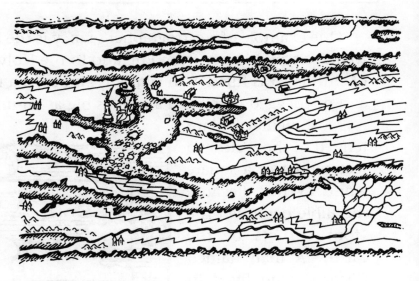

The World, the Middle Ages: Medieval mapmakers and tour guides drew up guidebooks to direct pilgrims to sacred places. Their maps depicted earth as circular, with Jerusalem at the center; east was at the top, along with the Garden of Eden. Sometimes Noah's Ark was shown perched atop Mount Ararat, which is in present-day eastern Turkey. Holy landmarks and historic sites, notated with teachings from the Bible, completed the picture.

Jacques Cousteau invented the SCUBA in 19**43**.

GEOGRAPHER'S HALL OF FAME
Martin Waldseemüller

*M*artin Waldseemüller's 4½-by-8-foot map, made in 1507, was the largest in its day. It was also the first map to use the name America, after the explorer Amerigo Vespucci, who nosed around the coast of Brazil. Vespucci called that land *Mundus Novus*, Latin for "New World."

One example of a cartographer's fancy is the Hereford map, showing how to make a pilgrimage from England to the Holy Land. Along with locations of shrines, it is filled with symbols and even a few mythical creatures, such as a one-legged man with a foot as big as an umbrella!

Most medieval maps tended to show either a rectangular or a square world. Why? Because the Bible described the "four corners of the earth." A man named Cosmas, who lived in the sixth century, went so far as to divide the earth and its inhabitants

into four sections: The Indians occupied the east, the Ethiopians the south, the Celts the west, and the Scythians the north. A raging ocean surrounded these lands. Beyond this ocean was another world, where Paradise was located. Nothing could live on the antipodes (the very opposite ends of

Lambert Glacier, the longest glacier in the world, is **44**0 miles long.

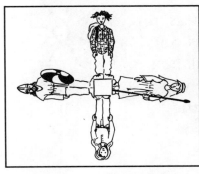

the earth), as explained by this riddle posed by Cosmas himself:

If two men on opposite sides of the earth placed the soles of their feet against each other, how could both be found standing upright?

Since no one could come up with a "logical" answer, the idea of a quadilateral, or four-sided, earth stuck, at least for a while.

Making Maps: How Did They Do It?

In order to make a useful map, people needed to know how far one place was from another. Before rulers, yardsticks, and measuring tape, people used lots of things to measure the distance between places.

HEY! I'M SUPPOSED TO BE TAKING EVEN STEPS FORWARD!

First they tried to measure the time it took for camels to walk a certain distance, but the camels didn't always cooperate. So they trained men, called bematists, to walk with perfectly even strides. Their steps added up to a stade, with one stade being about 606 feet. Ten stades—the length of 10 stadiums (think football fields) side by side—is approximately 1 mile. Later, *surveyors*, people who take measurements of places, got even more sophisticated and unwound huge chains, laying them flat to mark distances.

Geodesy, the branch of mathematics concerned with calculating the real shape of the earth, was introduced in the seventeenth century. Surveyors

BRAIN BUSTER

Look! California!

Only one country begins with the letter O. What is it?

Europe contains **45** countries.

were then using a tool called a **theodolite**. By measuring distances and angles with the theodolite, surveyors could measure the land by means of **triangulation**. Triangulation is based on simple geometry, which says that if you know the length of one side of a triangle and the measurements of the angles formed by the two adjoining sides, you can work out the lengths of the two remaining sides.

Mapmaking didn't change much until the 1930s, when air flight gave rise to **photo-grammetry**, a photographic technique that uses special cameras to make detailed maps from the air of areas impossible to survey on foot. When photographs taken from these cameras are laid on top of one another, the resulting picture appears three-dimensional. No 3-D glasses needed!

Surveyors measured the length of one side of a triangle with bematists. They figured out two angles using the sun.

GEOGRAPHER'S HALL OF FAME

Louise Arner Boyd

San Francisco socialite Louise Arner Boyd played an important role in the exploration of the Arctic Circle. One of the early pioneers of photogrammetry, her photo-grammetric surveys of the Franz Joseph Fjord along the 74th parallel in the 1940s enabled cartographers to map glaciers never before seen. Later, in the 1950s, she became the first woman to fly over the North Pole.

The wettest place in the world is Mawsynram, in India, with over **46**7 inches of rain a year!

THE PHANTOM CONTINENT, ANTARCTICA

Before the 1800s, mapmakers and geographers felt there must be a huge continent at the south end of the planet, just to keep things evenly balanced. *Terra Australis Incognita,* or "unknown southern land," was the name Ptolemy gave to the mysterious giant landmass that supposedly kept the earth from careening off its axis. Maps through the centuries showed this continent floating about the bottom of the earth. Some attached it to Africa, completely enclosing the Indian Ocean. The Russian Fabian Gottlieb Bellingshausen, Englishman Edward Bransfield, and American Nathaniel Brown Palmer all claimed to be the first to sight *Terra Australis Incognita* (Antarctica) in 1820.

Mapping Today . . . and Tomorrow

In the past, explorers traveled to distant lands, then mapped them out. Today we are mapping out places we've never been to at all—and doing it more accurately than ever.

Satellites can give us information hidden from view—on remote mountain ranges, impenetrable jungles, and even the ocean floor. They also help us learn more about our earth by showing us images in different forms. Right this minute, 22,000 miles above the equator, a system of 24 satellites is taking pictures of our earth—maybe of your backyard!

The NAVSTAR Global Positioning System, or GPS, orbiting more than 12,000 miles on average above the earth, provides some of the coolest maps today. By using the coordinates from GPS, dispatchers can alert the ambulance driver closest to the scene of an accident or the emergency truck

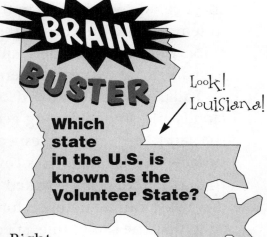

BRAIN BUSTER

Which state in the U.S. is known as the Volunteer State?

Look! Louisiana!

Indonesia has more islands than any other country—13,000 islands within 3,479 miles.

BRAIN BUSTER

Look! New Jersey!

Which state was named after Louis XIV, king of France?

nearest to a broken water main. It can also give sailors lost at sea a fix on their position or frustrated commuters a quick route out of a traffic jam. How does this work? Let's say you took a walk with a special handheld receiver. You could find out your location, speed, and altitude, thanks to signals you sent that bounced back to the receiver from three or more of the 24 GPS satellites orbiting the earth. Think of these signals, called waypoints, as a crumb trail, just like the one Hansel and Gretel left behind as they wandered through the forest. From your crumb trail, or waypoints, your receiver traces your route as you stroll along—so forget about using getting lost as an excuse for missing dinner ever again!

Heat-sensing devices in some satellites located miles out in space can detect changes in the temperature of the earth's oceans. Differences in temperature on earth, either on land or in the ocean, show up as different colors on a computer-generated map. These satellite images enable scientists to map global weather patterns, ocean currents, and wind currents.

Radar devices mounted on airplanes or satellites are able to penetrate clouds and smog, helping geographers observe the way people make use of the land they live on, especially in big cities like Los Angeles. Freeways, surface streets, high-rises, even the kinds of cars parked in driveways can be mapped for all to see. At the same time, special cameras and telescopes in space are sending back fascinating information about the far edges of our solar system, including images of the cloud patterns over Jupiter's moons.

FAR-OUT FACTOID

Quasars, which many astronomers believe to be small, active galaxies, are used as fixed points in modern mapping systems, because they are so distant they appear to never move.

The deep ocean current called the Gulf Stream is **48** miles wide and 2,100 feet deep.

Making It Fit: Map Projections

Here's a little mind-bender: Take a sphere—you know, a 3-D circle, a ball—and try to lay it flat. Don't just squash it; actually try to show all of it, laid out on a flat surface. How, you say? That is exactly the problem that faced one of the greatest mapmakers of all time, Gerardus Mercator. Back in the sixteenth century, he tried to transfer all the information of the earth's spherical surface onto a flat map and came up with a map projection. Of course to do this, a few little adjustments, such as splitting the oceans in half and stretching out Antarctica until it filled the entire bottom of the planet, had to be made.

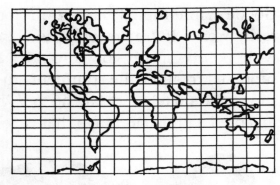

Mercator map projection

To preserve the shapes of the earth's oceans and landmasses, the Mercator map projection shows all lines of longitude as parallel but increases the distance between the lines of latitude the farther they are away from the equator. The northern and southern areas on Mercator projections therefore look a lot bigger than they really are. For instance, Greenland looks larger than South America, but in reality, the size of South America is eight times greater than the size of Greenland. (Check an atlas to compare the square mileage of both areas.) Since Mercator, there have been many kinds of map projections, all of them changing, or distorting, the shape of the continents and the oceans in some way.

Orthographic projections show shapes on earth as they would appear from space. Polar projections show either the North or South Pole. Equal-area projections do not

Look! Georgia!

BRAIN BUSTER

Which country in Africa has three capital cities?

Orthographic projection

The Dzungarian Desert in China is the farthest point on earth from an ocean—1,490 miles.

distort the size of the continents or oceans but do distort their shapes. A Goode's Interrupted Projection looks really weird. It "interrupts" the oceans with pointy spaces, or gores. This is supposed to allow the continents to be shown accurately. So far, no one has invented a projection map that is perfectly accurate.

Goode's Interrupted Projection

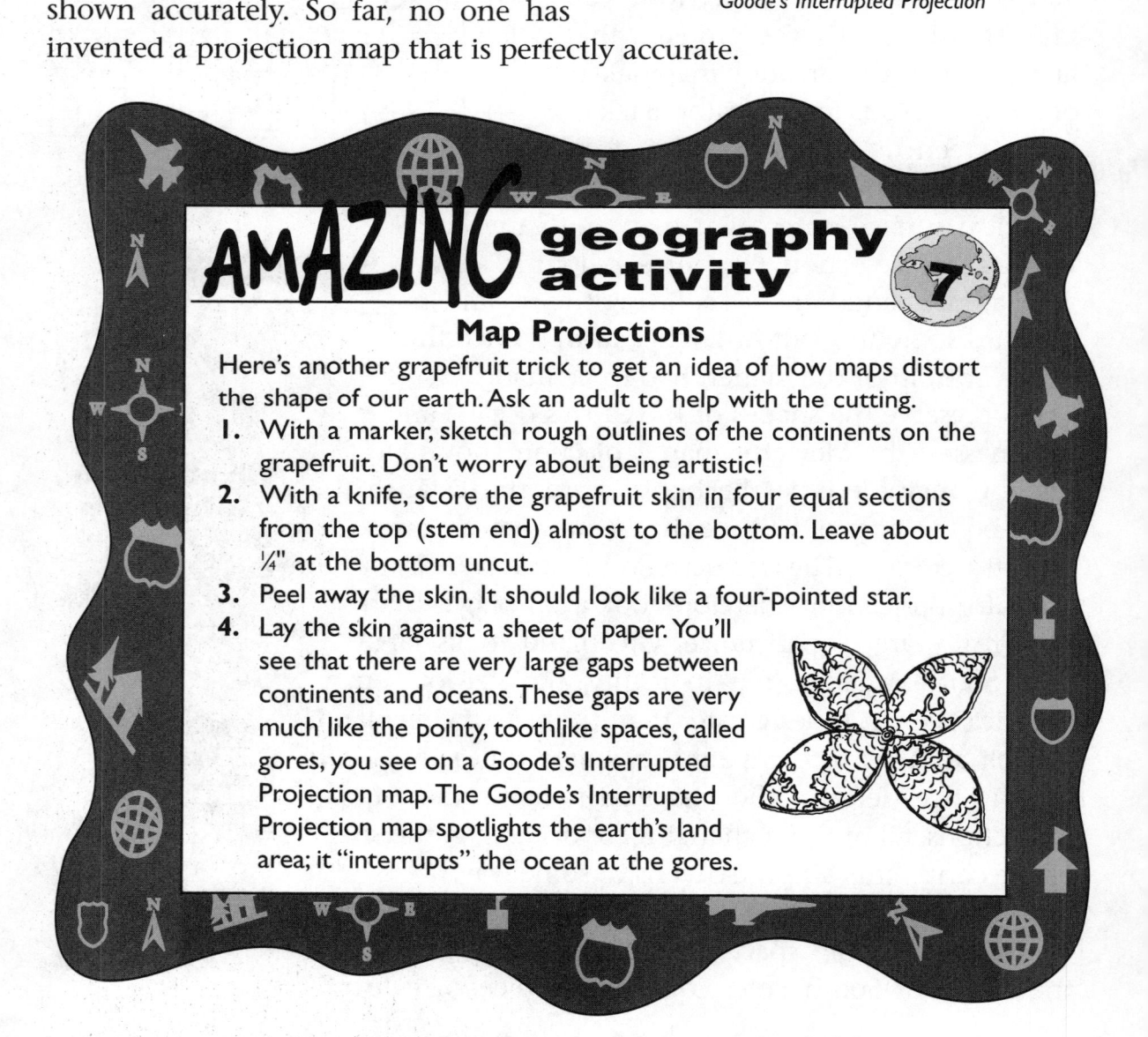

AMAZING geography activity 7

Map Projections

Here's another grapefruit trick to get an idea of how maps distort the shape of our earth. Ask an adult to help with the cutting.

1. With a marker, sketch rough outlines of the continents on the grapefruit. Don't worry about being artistic!
2. With a knife, score the grapefruit skin in four equal sections from the top (stem end) almost to the bottom. Leave about ¼" at the bottom uncut.
3. Peel away the skin. It should look like a four-pointed star.
4. Lay the skin against a sheet of paper. You'll see that there are very large gaps between continents and oceans. These gaps are very much like the pointy, toothlike spaces, called gores, you see on a Goode's Interrupted Projection map. The Goode's Interrupted Projection map spotlights the earth's land area; it "interrupts" the ocean at the gores.

The United States are made up of **50** states.

Even More Way-Out Web Sites

Here are some real places you can visit—as long as you have permission from your parents and access to a computer and the Internet:

- Need a map quick? Check out Mapquest for a map made just for you:

  http://www. mapquest.com

- The coolest sites around the Web these days are "instant cam" sites. For "live" video images of the coolest surf spots around the world, check out Leonard's Cam World at:

  http://www. leonardsworlds.com

GEOGRAPHY GOSSIP!

The story of Prester John and his holy kingdom was one of the longest-running rumors in history. Prester John, or Priest John, was supposedly a priest-king whose kingdom lay at the edge of the world. In the twelfth century, word spread that Prester John's city lay east of Persia (modern-day Iran). As more of the eastern world was explored (and nobody actually found Prester John or his kingdom), the location of Prester John's empire moved farther eastward or deeper into the African continent, depending on the storyteller. While no one ever discovered the location of Prester John's fabulous empire, the legend tempted many to pull on their traveling boots. In the process, much of western Africa was explored.

In 1513, V. Nuñez de Balboa became the first European to see the Pacific Ocean.

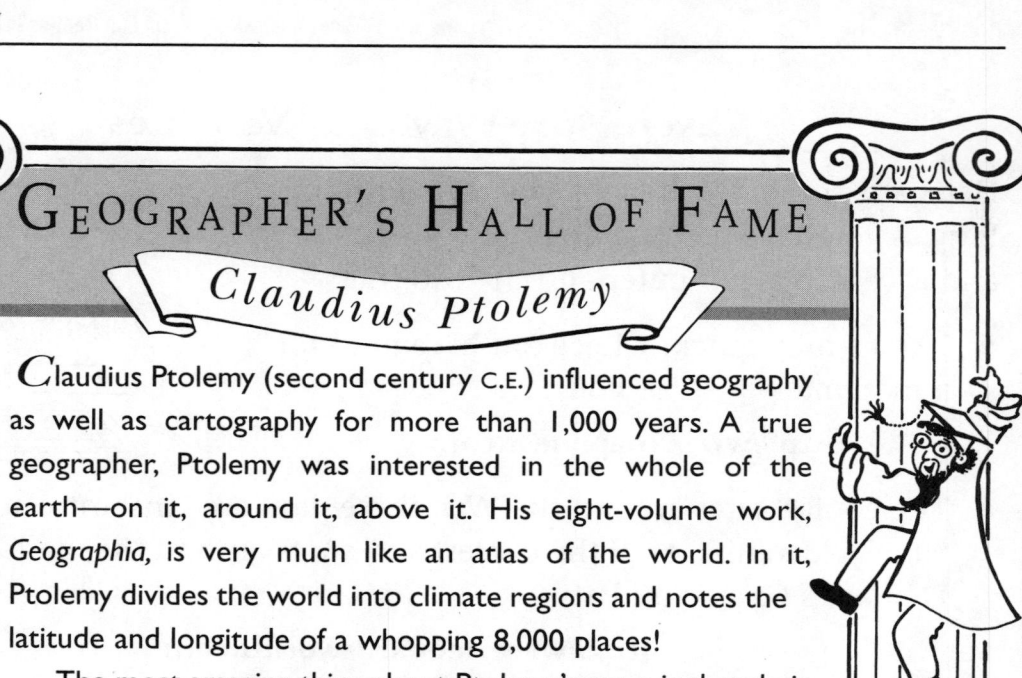

GEOGRAPHER'S HALL OF FAME
Claudius Ptolemy

Claudius Ptolemy (second century C.E.) influenced geography as well as cartography for more than 1,000 years. A true geographer, Ptolemy was interested in the whole of the earth—on it, around it, above it. His eight-volume work, *Geographia,* is very much like an atlas of the world. In it, Ptolemy divides the world into climate regions and notes the latitude and longitude of a whopping 8,000 places!

The most amazing thing about Ptolemy's maps is that their basic format is still followed today. For instance, Ptolemy was probably the first to orient maps with the north at the top and the east to the right. His system of legends and symbols, as well as instructions for map projections, continued to be used by cartographers more than 1,000 years later.

Explorers also used Ptolemy's maps. However, the one big mistake Ptolemy made was his estimation of the size of the earth and its oceans. Ptolemy figured the earth was smaller than it actually is, which made things quite interesting for sailors, including Christopher Columbus.

Look! Idaho!

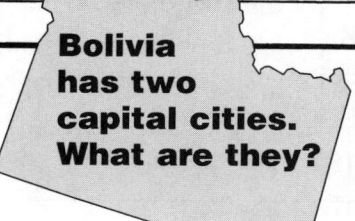

BRAIN BUSTER

Bolivia has two capital cities. What are they?

Africa contains **52** countries.

CHAPTER 4

IT'S A COOL, CHANGING WORLD: THERE'S SOME SERIOUS MOVING GOING ON!

Earth has not always been seven continents separated by lots and lots of water, the way we know it right now. All during its long history, the earth has been restless. Tremendous forces beneath the surface have shaken up the oceans, split continents, and squeezed mountains. In fact, at one time, the continents were probably all linked as one giant landmass. But, whoa! Let's back up a minute and take a here-and-now look at this big ole planet we call home.

As fearless geographers, we'll hurtle through the earth (down, down, down . . .) and check out what's at its very center. So trade in your grapefruits for an egg—one that's a bit rounder than your average ostrich egg—and let's compare the earth to it.

Just like the egg's shell, the earth's crust is hard and crunchy. This crust is about 2 miles thick under the oceans and more than 50 miles thick under the mountains. But unlike the egg shell, the earth's crust is not one solid piece. No, it is made up of large masses of rock, called *plates*. Some of these plates support the continents; others support the oceans. The plates themselves float over a thick layer of

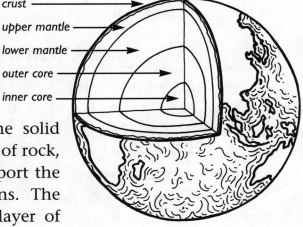

crust
upper mantle
lower mantle
outer core
inner core

The world's deepest lake is Lake Baikal in Siberia, which goes down **5,3**71 feet at its deepest point.

BRAIN BUSTER

Look! North Dakota!

The deepest drilled hole—a little more than 7½ miles in depth—was made by a scientific exploration team in Russia. Its exact location is at 67° N, 37° E. Can you find the place?

superheated rocks and *magma*, or melted rock. (Think of the runny white part of the egg!) This 1,800-mile-thick layer is called the *mantle*.

About 45 miles inside the mantle, things get pretty wild. When magma and rock squeeze through a hole or crack in a plate above, one of earth's most violent and spectacular shows occurs—a volcano. Below all this raging activity is the earth's core: in egg terms, an egg yolk, but in earth terms, a superhot ball of rock.

Again, above the core and mantle, the plates of the earth's crust float about on a lake of superheated rock and magma. Like a huge bumper boat, each plate is constantly jostling for position, pressing past one plate, crushing against another. The movement of these plates and all the activity underneath them is called *plate tectonics*. Many branches of science have contributed to our current knowledge of plate tectonics: paleontology, the study of fossils; geology, the study of the physical history of the earth; and seismology, the study of earthquakes. Plate tectonics has shaped the earth in fantastic ways—some you can see and experience right now, others that happened millions of years ago.

Once Upon a One-Land Planet

If you've noticed that South America and Africa look like mirror, or reverse, images of each other, you're not alone. Many people noticed this back when the first world maps were made, including the famous mapmaker Abraham Ortelius in 1587. In his *Thesaurus Geographicus,* Ortelius argued that the continents were once joined. He wrote that the Americas were "torn away" from Europe and Africa by earthquakes and floods. They have since wandered apart.

The Amazon River got its name from the female warriors who attacked explorer Francisco de Orellana, as he sailed the river in 1541.

Others had similar ideas, but the concept of wandering continents did not have a name until 1912, when 32-year-old meteorologist Alfred Lothar Wegener unveiled his own theory and called it **continental drift** (you know, as in continents that drift!).

Wegener theorized that about 200 million years ago, the earth was covered by one huge ocean as well as one huge continent called Pangaea (which means "all earth" in Greek). Gradually, this supercontinent split into two large landmasses: Laurasia in the Northern Hemisphere and Gondwanaland in the Southern Hemisphere. As Laurasia and Gondwanaland continued to break off into smaller pieces, some pieces of land clung to each other by thin fingers. Two such areas are the **isthmus** of Panama, which bridges North America and South America, and the isthmus at Suez in North Africa. (As you may have guessed, an isthmus is a narrow strip of land that connects two larger areas of land.) Other odd-looking land shapes began to form, too, such as peninsulas (land surrounded on three sides by water).

approximately 200 million years ago

landmass gradually separated

earth today

Proving the Drift

To support his continental drift theory, Wegener showed that the mountain ranges of the continents of Africa and South America are the same type and age. Not only that, but rocks found on the west coast of Africa and the east coast of South America were similar. Fossils of certain species of plants and animals found on them were also the same. How could this be? The ocean separating the two continents was too large for these ancient life forms to simply jet from one to the other. The most likely solution to the mystery? The two continents were attached at some point in the past.

The longest mountain chain is the Andes in South America at **5,5**00 miles long.

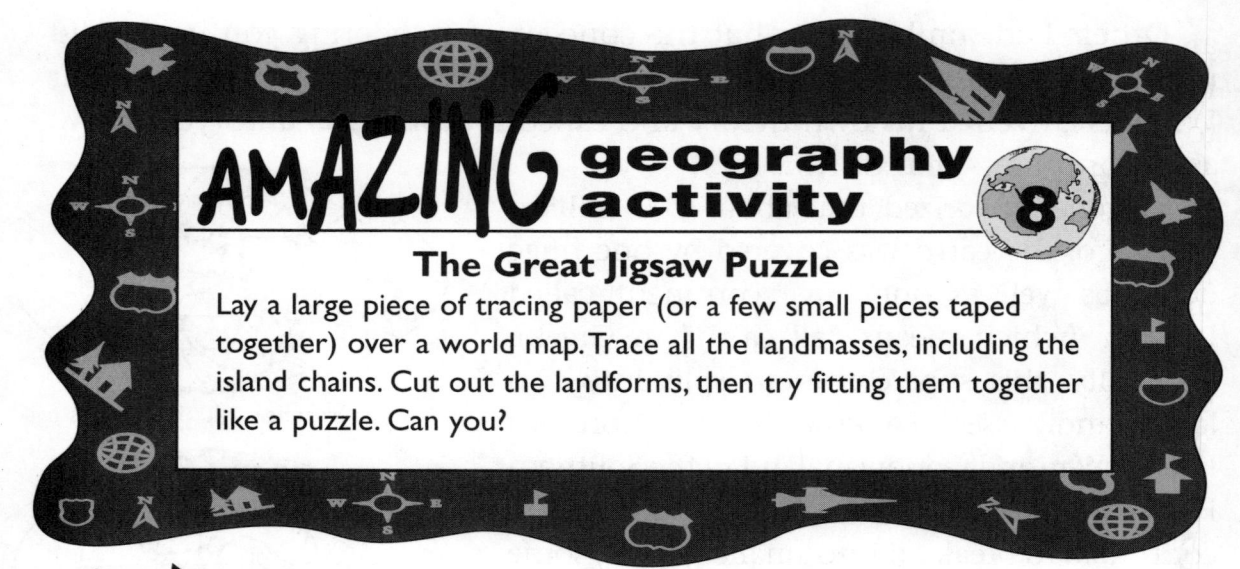

AMAZING geography activity

8

The Great Jigsaw Puzzle

Lay a large piece of tracing paper (or a few small pieces taped together) over a world map. Trace all the landmasses, including the island chains. Cut out the landforms, then try fitting them together like a puzzle. Can you?

BRAIN BUSTER

You'll need to get out your maps to solve this one: Where in South America can you be only 30 miles from the equator but knee-deep in snow?

Look! Arizona!

Wegener suggested that the continents moved along the ocean floor, but no one could imagine such huge landmasses moving at all. So people called Wegener's ideas about continental drift preposterous. Now, if people called your ideas preposterous, what would you do? Why, prove your ideas right! And that's exactly what Wegener set out to do. He spent the rest of his life looking for more evidence to prove his theory. But not until after his death in 1930 did such evidence come to light—all the way from the ocean floor.

That Busy Ocean Floor!

When the ocean floor was just beginning to be mapped in the 1950s and 1960s, scientists found huge undersea mountain ranges, the longest on the planet. Called the global mid*ocean ridge* system, these mountains snake

The **5,6**00-mile Silk Road was the greatest long-distance trade route ever.

around the globe like the seam on a baseball. And they are higher than any mountain in the United States—except Mt. McKinley in Alaska, which rises to 20,320 feet.

When oil companies began drilling deep into the ocean floor after World War II, more information about the world hidden beneath the earth's crust was revealed. For example, it was discovered that the plates under the Atlantic Ocean are moving away from each other *verrry slooowly*, widening the Atlantic. Spreading plates had already been responsible for

tearing Saudi Arabia away from the African continent, forming the Red Sea. A rift, where plates are being pulled apart, is also tearing eastern Africa away from the rest of the continent. Near Ethiopia, geologists have observed sea water from the Indian Ocean seeping inland along cracks separating the plates. They are witnessing the birth of a new sea that will eventually turn the horn of Africa into a large island.

A Collision of Plates

Now you know what happens when plates move away from each other. But what happens when plates move *toward* each other? The Himalaya mountain range shows dramatically what happens when one continental plate won't budge for another.

Imagine you're at a dessert bar. At the far end, you spy a delicious-looking chocolate mousse cake. "I'll have that one," you call to the waiter, who slides the cake down the counter, aiming for your outstretched hands. But at that moment, Harold, the busboy who is a weight

Together, all of earth's landmasses equal **57**,821,000 square miles in area.

lifter in his spare time, leans his bulging biceps against the very same counter. The chocolate mousse cake meets an immovable object, and *splat*! The mousse cake has nowhere else to go but up!

When the plate supporting India and the plate supporting Asia met in a spectacular head-on collision, the Eurasian plate (the plate carrying Europe and Asia) squashed upward like that chocolate mousse cake, forming the Himalayas, now the highest continental mountain range in the world. And the plates are still pushing against each other, causing this range to grow more than 3.3 feet every thousand years. (But who's keeping count?)

The Ring of Fire

The Ring of Fire is home to the world's most active volcanoes and destructive earthquakes. Unlike any ring you've ever seen before (i.e. onion ring, circus ring, nose ring), the Ring of Fire winds in a huge arc in the Pacific Ocean through Micronesia, China, Japan, and Eastern Russia over to Alaska and the western United States and South

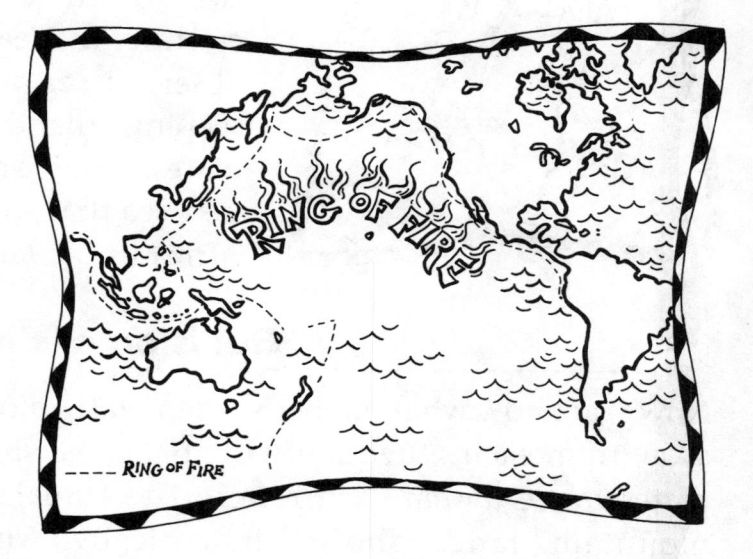

America. How did the Ring of Fire become such a quaking and shaking area, as well as a risky vacation spot? Plate movements again, but this time of a different nature.

Here goes: The plate supporting the Pacific Ocean (the Nazca plate), which is heading east, is being forced under the South American continental plate, which is drifting west. The result? Deep ocean trenches on one side of the Nazca plate and the Andes Mountain chain on the other. It's all this pushing and tugging at the edges of these plates that causes the Ring of Fire.

The center point of all 50 U.S. states is Castle Rock, South Dakota, at 44°58' S by 103°46' W.

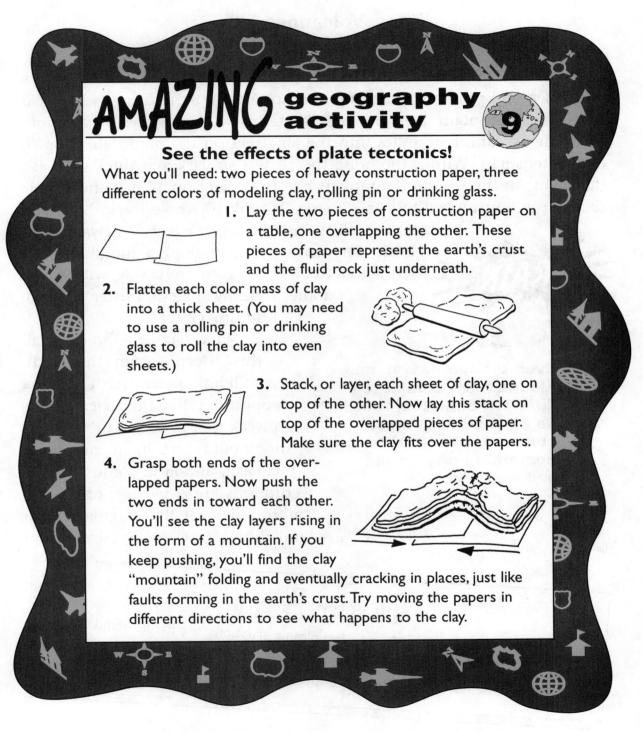

AMAZING geography activity 9

See the effects of plate tectonics!

What you'll need: two pieces of heavy construction paper, three different colors of modeling clay, rolling pin or drinking glass.

1. Lay the two pieces of construction paper on a table, one overlapping the other. These pieces of paper represent the earth's crust and the fluid rock just underneath.

2. Flatten each color mass of clay into a thick sheet. (You may need to use a rolling pin or drinking glass to roll the clay into even sheets.)

3. Stack, or layer, each sheet of clay, one on top of the other. Now lay this stack on top of the overlapped pieces of paper. Make sure the clay fits over the papers.

4. Grasp both ends of the over-lapped papers. Now push the two ends in toward each other. You'll see the clay layers rising in the form of a mountain. If you keep pushing, you'll find the clay "mountain" folding and eventually cracking in places, just like faults forming in the earth's crust. Try moving the papers in different directions to see what happens to the clay.

Tsunamis can travel across the ocean as fast as **59**7 miles per hour.

Volcanoes:
Earth's Builders and Movers

On May 18, 1980, Mount St. Helens in Washington State turned from a quiet, peaceful peak into a boiling inferno. After waking from its 123-year sleep, the mountain blew its top (literally) with a violent explosion, throwing ash and rock miles into the air. Trees on the mountain toppled like matchsticks. Within the hour, the air was so dark and thick with ash that lights in the surrounding towns had to be kept on all day and people couldn't go outside without face masks. It took 10 whole weeks to finally haul away all the ash from city streets, sidewalks, and roofs. The once perfectly sloping mountain was left with a tremendous gash on its side, with a new dome forming like a blister on the resulting crater.

What happened to cause all this? Deep within the earth, colliding plates push magma upward. When this magma finds a weak spot in the earth's crust, it shoots out from it in an eruption of rock, ash, and *lava*. Some volcanic eruptions are explosive; others are more sedate. If the magma is thin and runny, gases easily escape from

BRAIN BUSTER

Even though Hawaii and Alaska have completely different climates, they do have something in common. What? (Hint: Something originating underground.)

Look! Oregon!

Far-Out Factoid

All of these places have been formed by volcanic eruptions: the Pacific island chain of Hawaii; the Aleutian Islands off Alaska; the Galapagos Islands of Ecuador, South America; and the Mariana Islands east of the Philippines.

The largest iceberg so far discovered is 208 miles long and **60** miles wide.

it and lava flows out of a volcano without much fanfare. (Fortunately, lava flows are slow moving and rarely kill people.) But if magma is thick and sticky, pressure builds up until the gases escape violently—and explode! The magma blasts into the air and breaks apart into pieces called *tephra*.

Also in the Ring of Fire is the big island of Hawaii, one of the most active volcanic islands on earth. Its gentle, if frequent, eruptions continue to add to that island's bulk. On the other side of the world, Iceland and its chain of volcanic islands are also constantly being reshaped by volcanic activity.

Look! Utah!

Look at a map of the United States. Can you figure out which mountains were called the Stony Mountains in the early 1800s?

In November 1963, cartographers had to get out their crayons and add another landmass (and name) to the world map, as a new island off Iceland emerged from the ocean during a huger-than-huge volcanic eruption. Over the next three-and-a-half years, the erupting volcano built up the island to 560 feet above sea level. Because this was a submarine volcano—an underwater volcano along the ocean floor—only about half of it showed above water. Today, U.S. and Icelandic geologists, biologists, and ecologists are crowded onto the one-square-mile island to conduct a long-term research project. They have named their workplace Surtsey Island, after Surt, the fire god of Icelandic mythology.

Earthquakes:
Earth's Movers and Shakers

Moving plates are also responsible for earthquakes. In a giant shoving match between plates deep beneath the earth's surface, the crust may buckle. When this happens along a crack, or *fault*, the stress shatters the

In 1616, English navigator William Baffin sailed into what is now known as Baffin Bay in Canada.

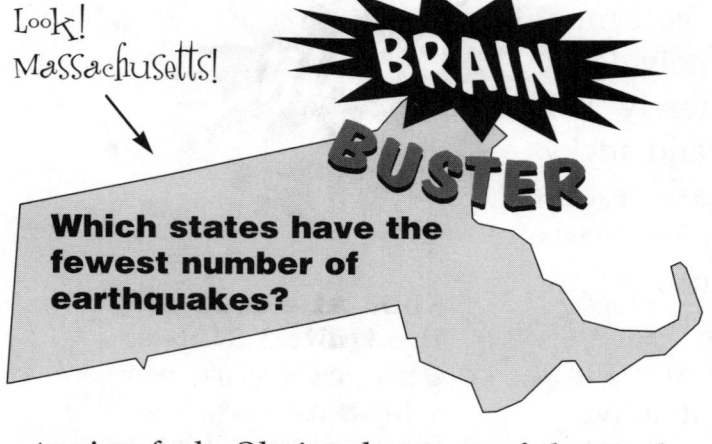

Look! Massachusetts!

Which states have the fewest number of earthquakes?

crust, whose rocky material then "snaps" into a new position. The shaking and rolling we feel on the surface are seismic waves, the vibrations created by all this shattering and shifting. These vibrations cause the entire planet (Yes, the *entire* earth!) to quiver like a giant tuning fork. Obviously, most of these vibes are not felt by anyone.

The most widely felt earthquakes in the recorded history of North America were the New Madrid, Missouri, quakes during the winter of 1811 to 1812. Earthquakes shook up the area in December, January, and most powerfully, in February. These earthquakes were felt by people as far east as Boston and as far west as Denver. (Some people say these quakes made the Liberty Bell in Philadelphia, Pennsylvania, ring!)

The Alaskan earthquake of March 27, 1964, was felt over an area of almost 500,000 square miles. The ground motion near the *epicenter*, the place where the earthquake is centered, was so violent that tree-tops snapped off.

Far-Out Factoid

Earthquakes beneath the ocean floor sometimes generate immense sea waves or tsunamis (meaning "huge wave" in Japanese). These waves can travel the ocean at speeds as great as 597 miles per hour and may rise as high as 50 feet (or higher) by the time they reach the shore!

One of the world's earliest geographers, Thales, lived from **62**5 to 547 B.C.E.

THE TOP MAGNITUDE EARTHQUAKES IN THE UNITED STATES

(measured on the Richter Scale*)

State	Date	Magnitude
⊕ Andreanof Islands, Alaska	3/09/1957	8.8
⊕ New Madrid, Missouri	1811–1812	8.8
⊕ Rat Islands, Alaska	2/04/1965	8.7
⊕ Shumagin Islands, Alaska	11/10/1938	8.3
⊕ Lituya Bay, Alaska	7/10/1958	8.3
⊕ Cape Yakataga, Alaska	9/04/1899	8.2
⊕ Yakutat Bay, Alaska	9/10/1899	8.2
⊕ Andreanof Islands, Alaska	5/07/1986	8.0
⊕ Fort Tejon, California	1/09/1857	7.9
⊕ Ka'u District, Hawaii	4/03/1868	7.9
⊕ Kodiak Island, Alaska	10/09/1900	7.9
⊕ Gulf of Alaska	11/30/1987	7.9
⊕ Owens Valley, California	3/26/1872	7.8
⊕ Imperial Valley, California	2/24/1892	7.8
⊕ San Francisco, California	4/18/1906	7.7
⊕ Pleasant Valley, California	10/03/1915	7.7
⊕ Kern County, California	7/21/1952	7.5

*Magnitudes are estimated based on intensity for earthquakes that occurred before 1938.

In 1632, French explorer Jean Nicolet explored Lake Michigan.

Measuring Earthquakes

An earthquake can be measured, and so described, by its intensity and magnitude. Intensity is based on how people, buildings, and the ground itself are affected by the shaking. Many intensity scales have been developed over the last several hundred years to evaluate the effects of earthquakes. The one currently used in the United States is the Modified Mercalli (MM) scale. This scale rates the "feel" of the earthquake, from a slight shaking (no sweat) to catastrophe. Each level is described by Roman numerals, *I* being the lowest and *XII* the highest. You could say that the Modified Mercalli is purely personal. In fact, after an earthquake hits, the U.S. Geological Survey mails questionnaires to area postmasters who then distribute them to the community, asking for people's opinions!

Magnitude, meanwhile, is based on the amplitude, or strength, of the seismic waves the earthquake produces. Seismic waves (remember: vibrations

The Most Intense Earthquakes in the World

(measured in Moment Magnitude)

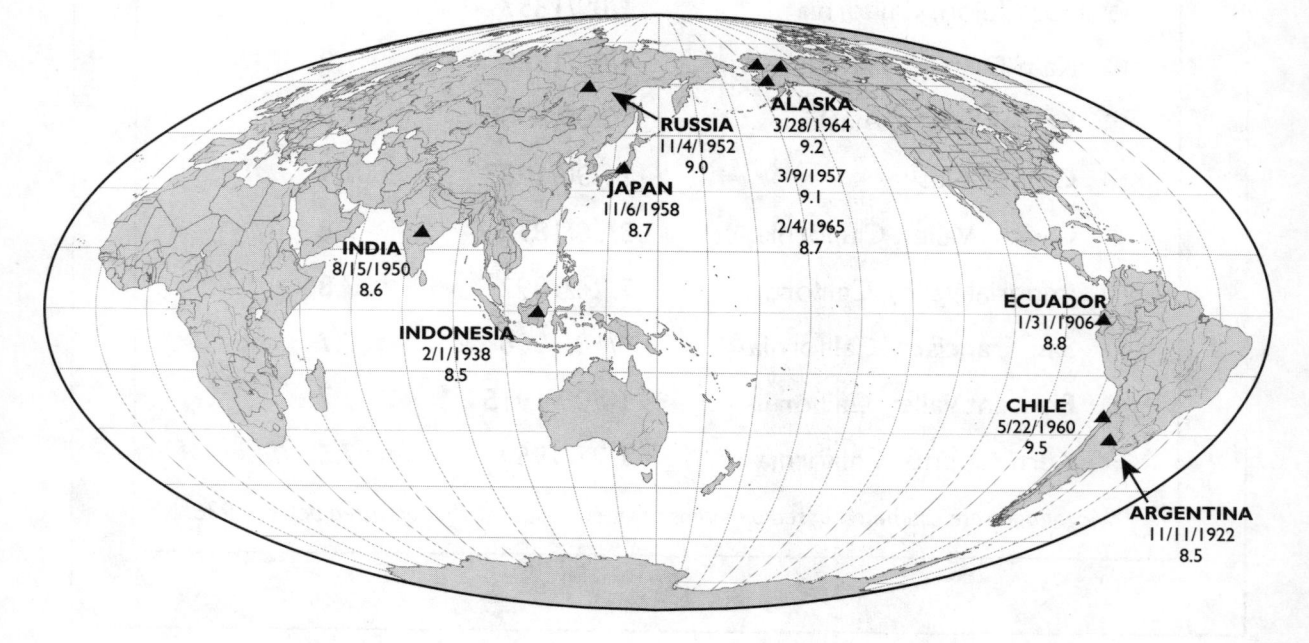

RUSSIA
11/4/1952
9.0

ALASKA
3/28/1964
9.2

3/9/1957
9.1

2/4/1965
8.7

JAPAN
11/6/1958
8.7

INDIA
8/15/1950
8.6

INDONESIA
2/1/1938
8.5

ECUADOR
1/31/1906
8.8

CHILE
5/22/1960
9.5

ARGENTINA
11/11/1922
8.5

New Zealand was sighted and named by Abel Janszoon Tasman in 1**64**?.

from earthquakes) travel through the earth. These waves, or vibrations, are detected, recorded, and measured by instruments called seismographs. The magnitude of seismic waves are measured by the Richter Scale, which runs from 0 to 9. Each number on the Richter Scale is 10 times greater than the number before it. That means a magnitude 7 earthquake is 10 times stronger than a magnitude 6 and 100 times stronger than a magnitude 5!

As you can see, very few great earthquakes occur in any given year:

Type	Magnitude	Average Annually
Great—total and major damage	8 and higher	1
Major—major damage	7–7.9	18
Strong—moderately destructive	6–6.9	120
Moderate—felt by everyone in vicinity and causing minor damage	5–5.9	800
Light—felt by most people in vicinity and causing slight damage	4–4.9	6,200 (estimated)
Minor—felt indoors	3–3.9	49,000 (estimated)
Very Minor—barely felt	2–2.9	about 1,000 per day
Very, Very Minor—detectable by instruments only	1–1.9	about 8,000 per day

Cool Shape-Shifters

Earthquakes and volcanoes aren't the only natural wonders that have shaped our world. During the earth's ice ages, the world looked very different. Glaciers, large masses of ice and snow, crept over most of the Northern Hemisphere. These slow-moving sheets of ice dragged rocks and earth along their path, carving bizarre designs in the land. The glaciers came and went several times until finally, about 10,000 years ago, they melted and formed the Great Lakes in the northcentral United States, as well as rivers like the

St. Augustine, Florida, founded in 15**65**, is the oldest U.S. town of European origin.

Mississippi. (Think Frosty the Snowman on a much, *much* larger scale.) The Devil's Tower in Wyoming is a souvenir from the most recent ice age. This lonely lump of rock stands 865 feet high!

Because most of the earth was covered in ice during the ice ages, scientists believe that the level of the oceans was once much lower. Many areas now covered by water may have, at one time, been dry land. It is believed that the Bering Strait, which separates Asia (Russia) from North America (Alaska), provided a kind of land bridge for people and animals thousands of years ago.

An ice age in the near future is not a worry; in fact, nobody knows when another one could occur. Many scentists do believe, though, that the earth may experience another ice age someday. Yikes! Better bring a sweater.

Still More Way-Out Web Sites

Here is a real place you can go—as long as you have permission from your parents and access to the Internet:

● Join the *Aquarius,* an undersea lab sponsored by the National Oceanographic and Atmospheric Administration (NOAA) and the National Underwater Research Program. Up to six scientists can live in this underwater habitat for a week. Look for photos and diary entries from the latest study off the coast of Key Largo, Florida:

http://www.noaa.gov

Route **66,** also known as "the Main Street of America," is 2,048 miles long and extends from Chicago, Illinois, to Santa Monica, California.

COOL WORLD, COOL PEOPLE: So Many Faces, So Many Places

Human beings have traveled all over the world—by car, boat, plane, train, motorcycle, hot-air balloon, and even dogsled. And wherever they've gone, they've had to adapt, or change, depending on the region where they've chosen to live. (A region is an area distinguished by certain characteristics.) Do you realize you do this, too? If you moved, say, from Greenland to Florida, you'd need to trade your woolen socks and boots for sandals. The first settlers from England to America, for example, had to change their diet as they came to rely on such "new" foods as corn and pumpkin, abundant in the New World.

Depending on where you move, you may even have to change the type of house you live in. Some Native Americans frequently moved from place to place, living in tepees, portable homes that could be quickly pulled down when needed. And if you were a pioneer on the *plains*, you might have made your home from sod blocks, because so few trees grew there!

All seven continents have a large variety of natural regions, with distinct characteristics, including climate, landforms, and animal and plant life.

BRAIN BUSTER

What's the largest country in the world?

Look! Connecticut!

The world's widest waterfalls, Khone Falls stretch **6.7** miles across the Mekong River.

Geographers divide the earth into the following natural regions:

- polar regions
- temperate forests and **grasslands** (prairies)
- **tropical rain forests**
- alpine (mountain) regions
- hot grasslands (savannas)
- deserts

Cultural regions, on the other hand, are distinguished by the people of the region and how they live—their language, religion, politics, industry.

There can be more than one cultural and natural region on one continent or in one country—even in one city, if you count neighborhoods as a type of region. You can learn a lot about the way people live by looking at where they live. So let's jump aboard . . . hey, how about that iceberg floating along? Grab your gloves, and we'll take a tour of this amazingly diverse planet and its regions. First stop: the "bottom" of the world, Antarctica.

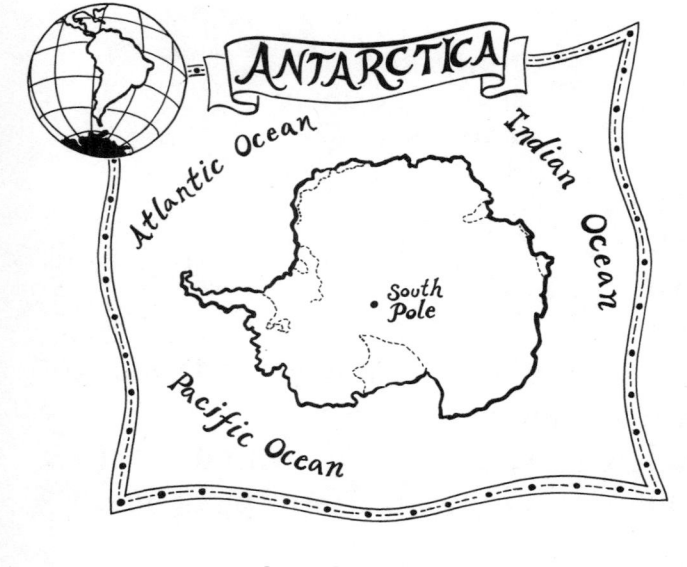

Antarctica, the World's Largest Refrigerator

Most of the world's largest icebergs originate on this refrigerated continent, which was also the last one discovered. Antarctica is a polar region, a desert with very little rainfall, because the air is too cold for clouds to form. Except for a bunch of shivering scientists, very few lifeforms make their homes there. But while

Ralph Plaisted reached the North Pole by snowmobile in 19**68**.

you'll find only a few mites and lichens on land, Antarctica's seas are rich with plant life, and whales and seals love its cold waters.

Because nothing much happens on Antarctica to disturb what's there, scientists have learned a lot about the history of the earth by drilling into its glaciers for samples of snow that fell thousands of years ago. We can even see the effect of human civilization thousands of miles away; for example, the snow in Antarctica gets dirtier the closer it is to the surface. Pretty amazing, huh? Winds have busily blown particles from smokestacks and factories around the world onto this snow-covered southern continent.

While you won't be affected by the pollution on this frozen continent, pollution in your part of the globe could cause all sorts of problems, including that sunburn on your nose! Freon, which is found in aerosol cans, refrigerators, and air conditioners, creates a pesky hole in the earth's atmosphere. This hole gives the sun's rays a pipeline straight to your nose (and other bare parts of your body).

> ### Far-Out Factoid
> About two-thirds of the world's population—that's 3.6 billion people!—live within 37 miles of a coast.

Next Stop . . . South America!

South America has almost every kind of natural region on earth. The world's longest mountain chain, the Andes, separates the continent, with tropical rain forests of Brazil to the east and Colombia to the north, and the deserts, mountains, grasslands, and temperate forests of Chile, Peru, and Ecuador to the west.

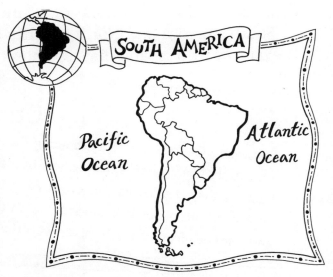

SOUTH AMERICA

Pacific Ocean

Atlantic Ocean

In 18**69,** the first expedition went through the Grand Canyon by way of the Colorado River.

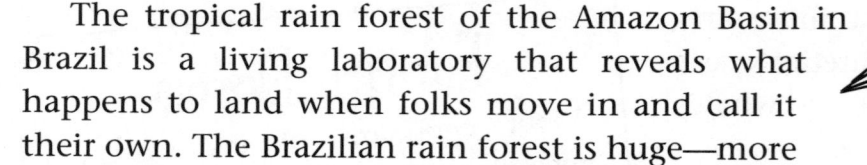

The tropical rain forest of the Amazon Basin in Brazil is a living laboratory that reveals what happens to land when folks move in and call it their own. The Brazilian rain forest is huge—more than 2½ million square miles in all. Unfortunately, every three seconds, a chunk the size of a football field is destroyed. The trees are disappearing as well as the animals that find shelter in and underneath them. Humans are responsible for this terrible destruction. At one time, people and the forest had a good working relationship. Human inhabitants killed animals only for food. Eventually, however, certain farmers moved in and set up a fast-buck farming system called "slash and burn."

Slash-and-burn farmers chop and burn down trees to fertilize the ground and produce fast-growing crops. Overused, the soil soon loses its fertility, and the farmers move on to new tracts of rain forest and repeat the process. If this kind of farming continues, scientists say that in just 80 years, all of the world's tropical rainforests will disappear!

You'll find that South America is also home to many cowboys. The temperate grasslands, or pampas, of Argentina are perfect for grazing animals. *Gaucho* is the South American term for the cowpokes who herd cattle across these vast tracts of prairie.

South America and North America are joined by the isthmus of Panama, the narrow strip of land that separates the Pacific

Far-Out Factoid

South and Central America are along the Ring of Fire, a volcanically active part of the earth. Many people make their homes at the base of these volcanoes—not because they like to live dangerously but because the land there is very fertile. Of course, a volcanic blast is devastating on the land at first. But over time, the sulfur and minerals from the ash mixes with the soil, creating perfect land for farming.

The largest lake in North America is Lake Superior, at 31,**70**0 square miles.

and Atlantic oceans. We could ride our iceberg through this isthmus at the Panama Canal, a man-made waterway—and sailor's shortcut—which links the Atlantic and Pacific Oceans.

North America, Rich with Variety

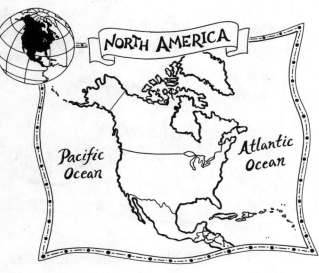

If you've ever traveled across the United States, Mexico, and Canada, you've seen a variety of regions, as well as people. About the only thing they all share is the same continent.

North America touches two oceans: the Atlantic on the east and the Pacific on the west. Mountain ranges snake across the edges of the continent. A ridge of aged mountain chains, the Appalachians, line the eastern section of the United States; in its western part, "younger" mountains, known as the Rockies, include Utah's Unta Mountains, New Mexico's Sangre de Christo Mountains, Colorado's Rockies, and California's

HOW THE FIRST AMERICANS INFLUENCED US

Some of the oldest place-names in the United States are from Native American languages. Check out the names of these states: Ohio ("great" in Iroquois), Michigan ("great water" in Chippewa), Massachusetts ("great hill, small place," named by the Massachusetts Indians), and Wyoming ("great plain," named by the Delaware Indians).

The MISSISSIPPI RIVER is the longest river in North America, at 3,710 miles long.

FAR-OUT FACTOID

One of the longest words in the world is *wiitokuchumpunkuruganiyügwivantümü,* which means "they who are going to sit and cut up with a knife a black female (or male) buffalo" in the Pauite language, spoken by Native Americans living in Utah, Arizona, Nevada, and California.

wiitokuchumpunkuruganiyügwivantümü

San Gabriels. The **continental divide**, formed by the Rockies, determines which way rivers flow. The waters that stream down its western slope run westward, making all the rivers that begin from those waters run in the same direction out to the Pacific Ocean; all the rivers formed from waters pouring down its eastern slope flow in the opposite direction, eastward, eventually out to the Atlantic.

The heartland of North America hosts the prairies . . . flatlands as far as the eye can see. The northernmost reach of North America is vast *tundra* and arctic desert, also known as the polar ice cap. Throw in some more deserts, a few white sand beaches, and Florida's famed swamps, the Okeefenokee, and you've just described the physical land of North America!

All this variety has made for an amazing mixture of people and cultures. Just in the United States

BRAIN BUSTER

What is a nickname for the Missouri River?

Look! South Dakota!

The United States Geological Survey was founded in 18**72**.

alone are these regions: the Northeast, Middle Atlantic, Southeast, Midwest, Southwest, West, and Northwest. Each region is distinguished by its location on the continent, its climates, and its industries, as well as its unique "state of mind," such as the laid-back feel of Southern California or the friendly hospitality of the Southern states.

Asia: The Biggest of Them All

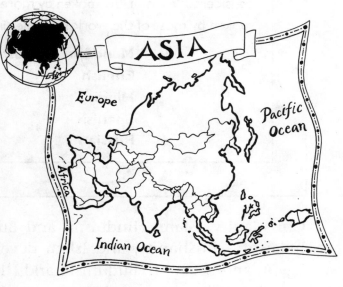

We'll have to leave our iceberg taxi behind now, because we can just about hop, skip, and jump westward across the Aleutian Islands to Siberia, the most northeastern region of Asia. Asia is the largest of all the continents. Plus it's attached to another continent, Europe. (In fact, some people lump Asia and Europe together and call the whole landmass Eurasia.) Most geographers consider the Ural Mountains a natural border between Europe and Asia, though the "official" border is man-made. (Just look at a political map.) Talking about mountains, Asia happens to have the highest and coldest in the world. Along with those mountains, forbidding deserts have helped to keep the people of the continent's different regions separated from one another.

The world's earliest civilizations developed separately though simultaneously along the Yellow River in China (the Far East) and along the Tigris and Euphrates River in Southwest Asia (the Near East, also called the Middle East). All the world's major religions—Judaism,

> ## Far-Out Factoid
> The 4,000-mile Great Wall of China is the only man-made structure on earth visible from space.

The first marine clock was completed in 1735 by John Harrison.

LANGUAGES OF THE WORLD

There are more than 200 main languages spoken on earth. (A language is considered "main" if it is spoken by more than 1 million people.) The languages spoken by most of the world's people (including natives and non-natives) are:

Mandarin Chinese	600,000,000
English	497,000,000
Hindi	394,000,000
Spanish	297,000,000
Russian	153,000,000

Christianity, Islam, Hinduism, and Buddhism—began in Southwest Asia. Judaism, Christianity, and Islam developed in what is now Israel, Syria, Egypt, and Lebanon. Buddhism and Hinduism started in India.

Asia also has a tremendous variety of written and spoken languages: There are six distinct language families spoken in Asia alone. Mandarin Chinese is not only the most common language spoken in Asia, it is also the language spoken by the greatest number of people in the world.

When ancient China needed more than the natural borders of the Gobi desert, the Taklimakan Steppes, and the Himalaya Mountains to separate those in the Far East from those in the Near East, the Great Wall of China was built. This construction project took almost 2,000 years to complete! It was begun in the third century B.C.E. and completed sometime during the Ming dynasty, 1368 to 1644.

BRAIN BUSTER

Which city in Germany was split in two at the end of World War II?

Look! Pennsylvania!

The Cambodian alphabet contains **74** letters—more than any other alphabet.

Europe: So Many Countries, So Little Time

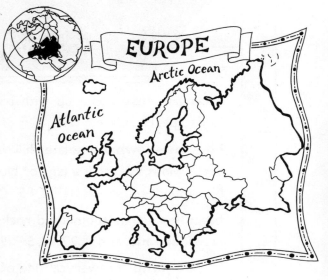

Europe has traded its lack of dramatic natural borders for a dazzling variety of political and cultural borders. Packed into a relatively small area, each country has developed its own culture.

In 1957, five European countries banded together to form the European Economic Community, or EEC. World War II had been devastating to many countries in Europe, and it was thought that economic cooperation would bring prosperity to the population. Since then, more countries have joined what is now called the European Union (EU). Included are France, Germany, the Netherlands, Belgium, Luxembourg, Austria, Italy, the United Kingdom, Ireland, Denmark, Sweden, Finland, Portugal, Spain, and Greece.

In a historic meeting in May of 1998, the European Union decided to create a common currency, where coins and money are worth the same amount in eleven of the EU's fifteen member countries. Unless things change, the *euro*, as this currency is called, should be in circulation by 1999. Many people think that the euro will help strengthen the European economy. But others will miss their familiar coins.

While it is the second smallest of the world's continents, Europe has the second largest population. Europe is best understood when you divide it into geographical/political regions.

The nations of northernmost Europe are identified as Scandinavia, which includes Norway, Sweden, Denmark, Iceland, and Finland. The countries of southern Europe—Italy, Spain, Portugal, and Greece—are dubbed the Mediterranean. Eastern European countries include, among others, Germany, Poland, Hungary, Slovakia and the Czech Republic, and Romania. Russia and its independent states are also considered part of Eastern Europe.

The first modern atlas was made in 13**75** for the King of Aragon in Spain.

LANDMARKS, CANADIAN-STYLE

Canadians have come up with some fanciful names for features of their landscape. Here are a few:

blow-me-down: An isolated hill rising steeply from the water and subject to fierce winds. We call it a *cliff* or bluff. (Look for the town of Blow Me Down, Newfoundland, at 49° 31' N, 55° 09' W.)

brandies: Partly submerged rocks, or a reef. (Look for Change Brandies, Newfoundland, at 49° 22' N, 54° 24' W.)

buffalo jump: The vertical side of a hill or river bank. A buffalo jump was a place where Plains Indians killed herds of bison by driving them over steep cliffs. (Look for Head-Smashed-In Buffalo Jump, Alberta, at 49° 43' N, 113° 39' W.)

mal bay: A tidal pond almost completely cut off from the sea by a sand bar. (Look for Windsors Mal Bay, New Brunswick, at 47° 57' N, 64° 29' W.)

pingo: A lone, ice-covered, cone-shaped mound appearing in areas of *permafrost*. (It's a cooler word than *mound, hill,* or *knoll.*) (Look for Ibyuk Pingo, Northwest Territories, at 69° 24' N, 133° 05' W.)

Russia, which is technically in Asia, and its independent states once belonged to the United Soviet Socialist Republic (U.S.S.R.). In 1991, the U.S.S.R. broke apart, making an impact felt around the world. Once a superpower and the largest communist country in the world, the Soviet government collapsed, and many parts of the old Soviet Union gained independence from the iron hand of communism. Russia has the distinction of having one foot in Europe and one foot in Asia. Western Russia, which includes the capital city of Moscow, butts up against Poland, the Baltic Sea, and the newly formed independent states of Estonia, Latvia, Lithuania, Belarus, Ukraine, Moldova, and Georgia. The vast lands of Siberia, east of the Ural

The largest inland sea or lake is the caspian sea at **76**0 miles long.

Mountains, stretch across Asia to the Bering Sea. Once a part of the U.S.S.R., the states of Kazakstan, Uzbekistan, Azerbaijan, Turkmenistan, Tajikstan, and Kyrgyzstan, cluster between the Asian countries of China, Iran, and Afghanistan.

Where is the "Roof of the World"?

Look! Wyoming!

The Scandinavians are a hardy people who have used the difficult landscape to their advantage, as this story about the folks on Heimaey Island, Iceland, shows.

When the Eldfell volcano (which means fire mountain, in Icelandic) erupted near the town of Vestmannaeyjar in 1973, the people pulled together to save their town from the volcano's destruction. Most of the island's 5,300 residents were evacuated to the mainland of Iceland as ash and tephra buried 70 houses in town. But when huge chunks of lava threatened to block the town's important fishing port, the Icelanders fought back—and won! They sprayed seawater on the lava to slow and stop its movement and it worked. Not only that, the people of Vestmannaeyjar actually used the volcano to their advantage. When they rebuilt the town, they used heat from the cooling lava to construct a heating system for the island!

A different, but no less difficult climate affects the hot, dry Mediterranean region of Europe. But instead of making the land work for them, the people living in this fragile environment almost ruined the area for good. Around the fifth century B.C.E., the local environmentalists of Plato's time were warning of bad times to come. Overgrazing by goats and sheep and deforestation by hungry Phoenician shipbuilders stripped the tall pine trees and oaks from the beautiful hills of Greece and turned the land into dry tracts of scrub and weeds. Although the land of the Mediterranean will never be lush again, new farming techniques, irrigation, and a program of replanting trees keep the land from washing away completely. The climate is wonderful for grape-growing, and winemaking has become an important industry in the Mediterranean.

Indonesia has **77** active volcanoes, more than any other country.

Stretching across the midsection of Europe is the European Plain, an area of low, rolling hills great for farming. It runs across France and Germany and ends at the Ural Mountains. This is Europe's most populated area.

North of the European Plain are the British Isles, made up of Ireland and the United Kingdom. Within the United Kingdom is Scotland, England, Wales, and Northern Ireland. Since the 1960s, Ireland has been divided into mainly Protestant Northern Ireland and the Independent Republic of Southern Ireland, a mainly Catholic nation. A ceasefire from the violent fighting between the two countries and religious groups in April 1998 resulted in a landmark treaty, which may eventually reunite this divided land.

Two mountain chains—the Pyrenees and the Alps—provide a dramatic border between France, the largest country of Europe, and its neighbors. France's wealthiest neighbor is the tiny country of Luxembourg, which along with Belgium and the Netherlands, is known as Benelux. This economic union was formed between these countries in 1948, after World War II.

Africa: Where Many Wild Things Are

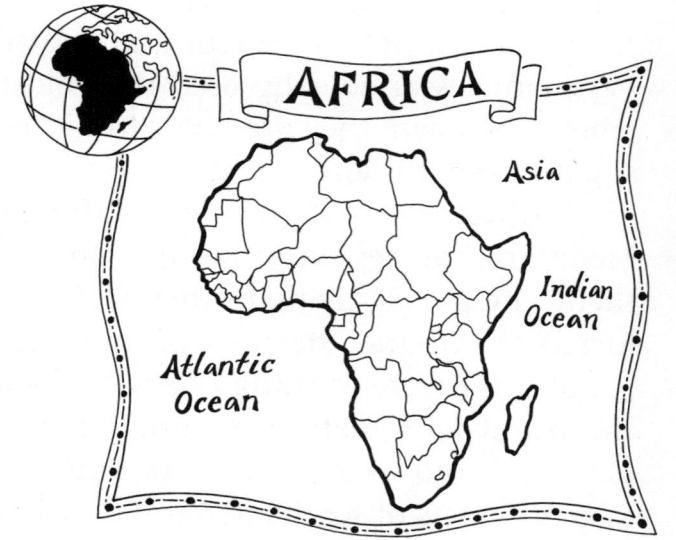

If you're surrounded by dry grasslands, as well as wildebeests, zebras, and lions, you're in the savannas that stretch from western Africa to the Great Rift Valley in eastern and southern Africa. If you're hot, humid, and hemmed in by crocodiles, you could very well be in the jungles of equatorial Africa.

The rugged landscape had kept people isolated, so local tribes developed their own languages and customs. In fact, there are more than 1,000 different languages spoken on the African continent, a land which was

longest railroad, the Trans-Siberian Railroad, stretches for 5,787 miles.

The World's

once colonized by people from Europe. When Europeans drew their own boundaries over this mosaic of countries, cultures, and languages in the eighteenth and nineteenth centuries, people and cultures clashed drastically.

How drastically? you wonder. Say you arrive at school in the morning and sit at your desk. You notice your teacher has been replaced. *A sub? Cool!* you think. But you quickly figure out that this teacher is no temp—when he hands out his list of rules 30 pages long—in a language you don't understand! Something like this happened to many of the people of Africa. They had their own languages, customs, and religious beliefs when suddenly they had to alter their whole way of life because strange new settlers took over their lands.

Even today, the continent of Africa continues to undergo change as people struggle to put the pieces of their homelands back together.

Far-Out Factoid

Thrifty, thirsty plants and animals in the Sahara Desert of northern Africa find enough water to survive just by absorbing the local fog!

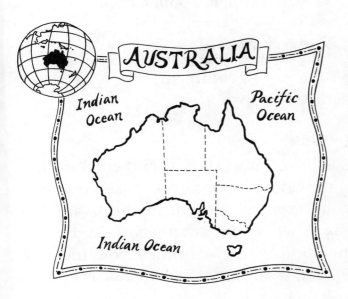

Australia: The Land Down Under

Australia, the smallest continent, is also the only continent besides Antarctica that is completely surrounded by water. Isolated by the Pacific Ocean, plant and animal life down under are like no others on earth: When was the last time you ran into a wombat?

The grasslands of southern Australia have their own version of the cowboy: Australian stockmen,

The world's deepest gorge is Hell's Canyon in Idaho, at **7,9**00 feet.

who herd sheep. (But don't call them sheepboys!) Another citizen of the Australian grassland is the kangaroo—the largest animal in the grasslands.

Most of Australia's population lives on the eastern edges of the continent, nice and close to the extraordinary Great Barrier Reef, the largest coral reef in the world. The Great Barrier Reef is one of the earth's natural wonders.

There's even a bit of skiing in Australia—just north of the island of Tasmania rise the Australian Alps. (So you can have your ski resort in Australia after all—just build it in the *southeastern* corner!)

Until the 1770s, the only humans living in Australia were the Aborigines, a hunting-gathering people who arrived there from Southeast Asia about 38,000 years ago. After Captain James Cook claimed the eastern coast of the island continent for Great Britain, Australia became that nation's dumping ground for convicts accused of such "terrible" crimes as stealing cheese or uprooting cucumbers. The number of these unwilling migrants grew quickly and they very soon outnumbered the Aborigine population.

Far-Out Factoid

The world's population is 5.8 billion (according to the *1998 World Almanac*) and growing at the rate of 1.6 percent a year. That's 180 babies born every minute!

But Wait . . . There's More!

While we've covered (so to speak) all the earth's continents, there are still many more places on the planet where people live.

Oceania: The Last to Be Discovered

More than 25,000 islands are sprinkled over most of the southern Pacific Ocean, from the Hawaiian Islands on the eastern end to Easter Island on the western end. These Pacific islands are grouped into three major areas: Polynesia, Micronesia, and Melanesia. Their island countries make up a region called Oceania. About eight million people live in these countries— that's slightly less than the population of Los Angeles alone! Because of their

In 1806, English whaler/scientist William Scoresby reached as far north as 81°21' north latitude—almost to the North Pole.

isolation, the islands of Polynesia, Melanesia, and Micronesia were the last places to be discovered by Westerners and the last islands to be populated by migration.

The Top of the World: The Arctic

The polar ice caps of the Arctic hardly seem a first choice for settlement. It's cold almost all the time, and there are no pineapple trees and very few movie theaters! And yet, the Eskimo people—the Lapps, Chukchi, Tungus, and Inuits—have adapted to their surroundings. In fact, Arctic dwellers have all developed similar techniques for survival. The sea provides food, fuel, and clothing in the form of seal meat, skin, and blubber. Even the Inuit boat of choice, the kayak, is made from the seal's waterproof skin.

Natives of the Arctic seem to be able to handle the fierce climate. In places like the frigid Kola Peninsula, the sun barely rises over the horizon for months at a time. Doctors have given a name to the constant headaches,

ANIMAL MIGRATIONS

Northern elephant seals migrate twice a year from Southern California to the North Pacific. Their trip averages 13,000 miles!

Like clockwork every winter, gray whales stream down the west coast of the United States from their homes in the Bering Sea to breed off the Baja coast of Mexico.

From 1811 to 1812, major earthquakes have shaken Missouri.

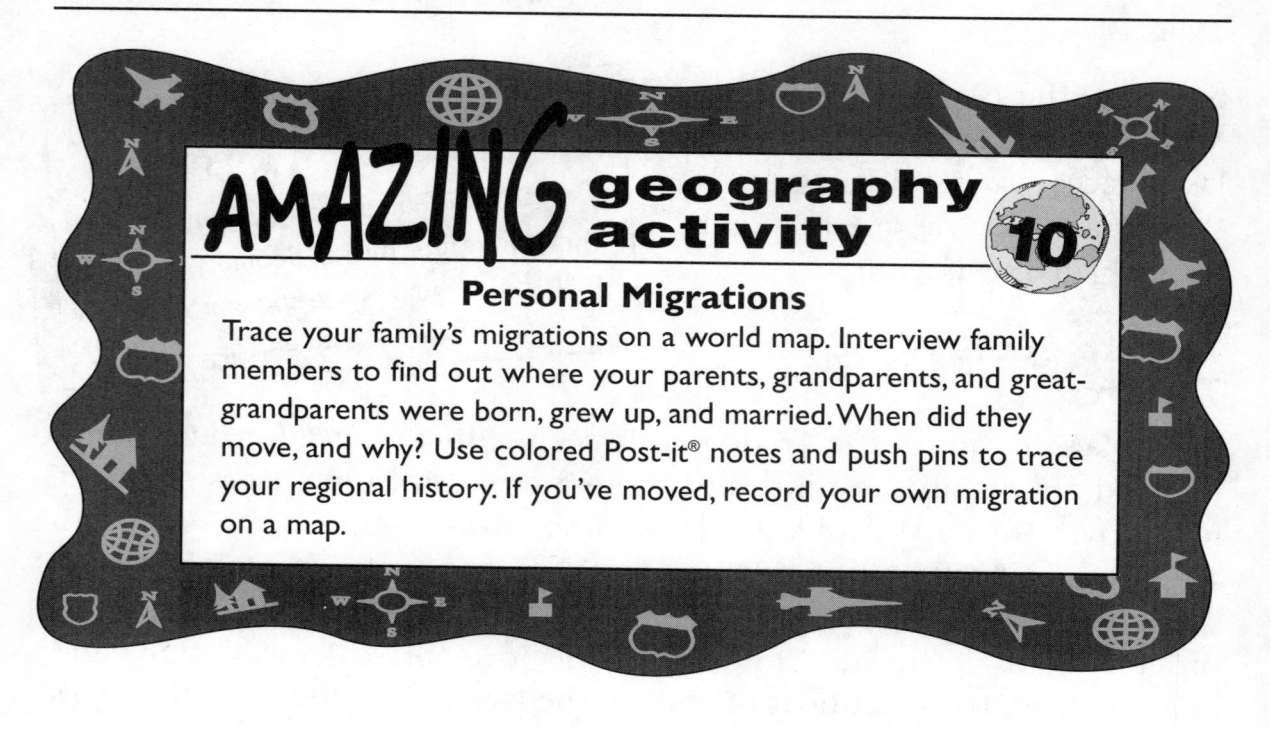

AMAZING geography activity 10

Personal Migrations

Trace your family's migrations on a world map. Interview family members to find out where your parents, grandparents, and great-grandparents were born, grew up, and married. When did they move, and why? Use colored Post-it® notes and push pins to trace your regional history. If you've moved, record your own migration on a map.

fatigue, and bad moods that plague folks who move to the frozen north from southern latitudes. It's called "polar night stress," and tanning salons, vitamin therapy, and artificially lit streets are just some of the things used to help non-natives cope with the long winters.

Cool Migrations: The Urge to Surge

People have been on the move for thousands of years. Have they moved for the fun of it? By mistake? Because they were greedy? People usually moved for the same reasons—to find a better place to live. Where they ended up in some cases depended on luck, climate, and technology.

People today are still migrating. They interact with their environment and change their surroundings in some way every day of their lives. When you or your friends travel from place to place and communicate with others, you exchange everything from music, language, ideas, and things you make. Cultures all over the world borrow from one another. For

The lowest point in North America is Death Valley, California, **282** feet below sea level.

instance, if you visit some foreign European country, like France (it could happen), you will find that most restaurants do not serve ice in their drinks. At first, you may find that awful, but by the time you get home, you just

① *Geographers think humans walked from Africa into Europe and Asia about 50,000 years ago.*

② *Those who moved east through Asia walked across the Bering Strait land bridge during the most recent ice age, about 15,000 years ago. (Remember, during the past ice ages, sea levels were much lower than they are now.)*

③ *Humans continued migrating until both North and South America were populated. By the 1400s, when Europeans came to the Americas, the Incas of Peru and the Aztecs of Mexico had been growing crops for more than 5,000 years!*

④ *The Indonesian* **archipelago** *might have provided stepping-stones to Australia for the ancestors of the Aborigines. Some people took to the seas from Australia and spread out to Samoa, Tonga, and even farther to Hawaii—distances of 5,000 miles or more.*

Out of every 100 people in the U.S., **83** have ancestors who came from Europe.

might be ordering "a Coke, hold the ice, please," at McDonalds™. Thus, a little bit of the European culture has rubbed off on you.

The Last of the Way-Out Web Sites

Here are some real places you can go—as long as you have permission from your parents and access to a computer and the Internet.

Since we can't actually hitch a ride on the next space shuttle, the Web is the next best thing to being there. Check out these sites, which include the latest, greatest images from space:

- Geography World is the gateway to a ton of wonderful Web sites really too numerous to mention. Sites about the world, natural wonders, cultures past and present, physical geography, and atlases are all included:

http://members.aol.com/bowermanb/101.html

- The Jet Propulsion Laboratory, or JPL, has a tremendous Web site. "Kidsat" gives you a chance to get involved:

http://kidsat.jpl.nasa.gov/
http://www.jpl.nasa.gov

- This cool Web site will take you to voyages and discoveries from the ancient to the present:

http://www.win.tue.nl/cs/fm/engels/discovery/index.html

Conclusion ... Let Your Exploration Continue

You've fallen through the earth, ridden on an iceberg, and hopped across islands in your quest to find the where and why of geography. But this is just the beginning. Are you jazzed about discovering how our earth works?

In 17**84,** the first map was completed through the process of triangulation.

Study up on volcanoes, earthquakes, and other natural forces that shape our world. Are there explorers who really fascinate you? Find out more about them! What continent do you most want to visit? Read about it—maybe even learn a language spoken there.

Whatever you do, don't stop exploring! Grab more grapefruits, make your own maps, and go and check out the world around you. Geography gives you the tools you need to observe and learn from this ever-changing world. You'll see that geography gets cooler and cooler the more you understand it!

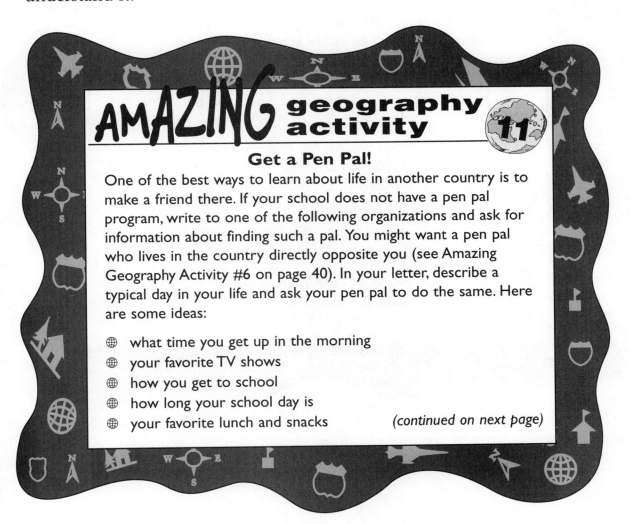

AMAZING geography activity 11

Get a Pen Pal!

One of the best ways to learn about life in another country is to make a friend there. If your school does not have a pen pal program, write to one of the following organizations and ask for information about finding such a pal. You might want a pen pal who lives in the country directly opposite you (see Amazing Geography Activity #6 on page 40). In your letter, describe a typical day in your life and ask your pen pal to do the same. Here are some ideas:

- ⊕ what time you get up in the morning
- ⊕ your favorite TV shows
- ⊕ how you get to school
- ⊕ how long your school day is
- ⊕ your favorite lunch and snacks

(continued on next page)

After being lost in fog, Bjarni Herjolfsson sighted North America around 9**85**.

Get a Pen Pal! *(continued)*

- your favorite recess activity
- what you have for breakfast
- what you have for dinner
- the names of your pets
- any brothers and sisters you might have
- how much homework you do
- how you and your friends celebrate birthdays
- what you like/what you dislike about school
- cool books you've read.

Here are pen pal organizations that will help you get connected with someone worldwide:

International Pen Friends
1308 68th Lane North
Brooklyn Center, MN 55430

Kids Meeting Kids
380 Riverside Drive, Apt. 8H
New York, NY 10025

Student Letter Exchange
308 Second Street NW
Austin, MN 55912

In 18**86,** France officially gave the Statue of Liberty to the United States.

ANSWERS

CHAPTER 1

BRAIN BUSTER, page 16: If you live on the East Coast of the United States, it's 16 hours ahead of you—actually, it's the next day!

BRAIN BUSTER, page 18: In water—the Atlantic Ocean, west of Africa, off the coast of Equatorial Guinea.

BRAIN BUSTER, page 20: A bathing suit. The seasons on the Southern Hemisphere are opposite those on the Northern Hemisphere.

AMAZING GEOGRAPHY ACTIVITY #3, page 20:
1. Maine.
2. Virginia and Michigan.
3. Colorado, Utah, New Mexico, and Arizona.

BRAIN BUSTER, page 21: Libreville, Gabon; Kampala, Uganda; Quito, Ecuador; Pontianak, Borneo.

CHAPTER 2

BRAIN BUSTER, page 24: The Straits of Gibraltar.

BRAIN BUSTER, page 30: Florida.

CHAPTER 3

BRAIN BUSTER, page 45: Oman.

BRAIN BUSTER, page 47: Tennessee.

BRAIN BUSTER, page 48: Louisiana.

BRAIN BUSTER, page 49: South Africa.

BRAIN BUSTER, page 52: La Paz, Sucre.

CHAPTER 4

BRAIN BUSTER, page 54: The Kola Peninsula.

BRAIN BUSTER, page 56: In Ecuador, on top of Cotopaxi, a volcano that, at over 19,000 feet high, has a nice little snowcap.

BRAIN BUSTER, page 60: Active volcanoes. This is because both states are positioned along edges of plates.

BRAIN BUSTER, page 61: The Rocky Mountains.

BRAIN BUSTER, page 62: Florida and North Dakota.

CHAPTER 5

BRAIN BUSTER, page 67: Russia.

BRAIN BUSTER, page 72: The Big Muddy.

BRAIN BUSTER, page 74: Berlin.

BRAIN BUSTER, page 77: Tibet, or Xizang (pronounced "shee-zang"), for its average elevation of close to 3 miles above sea level.

The smallest country in the world is Vatican City State in Europe— It's 108.7 acres!

Geography History at a Glance

B.C.E.

| 50 thousand years ago | 550 | 350–300 | 200 | 138 | 25 | 200 | 300–800 | 800 |

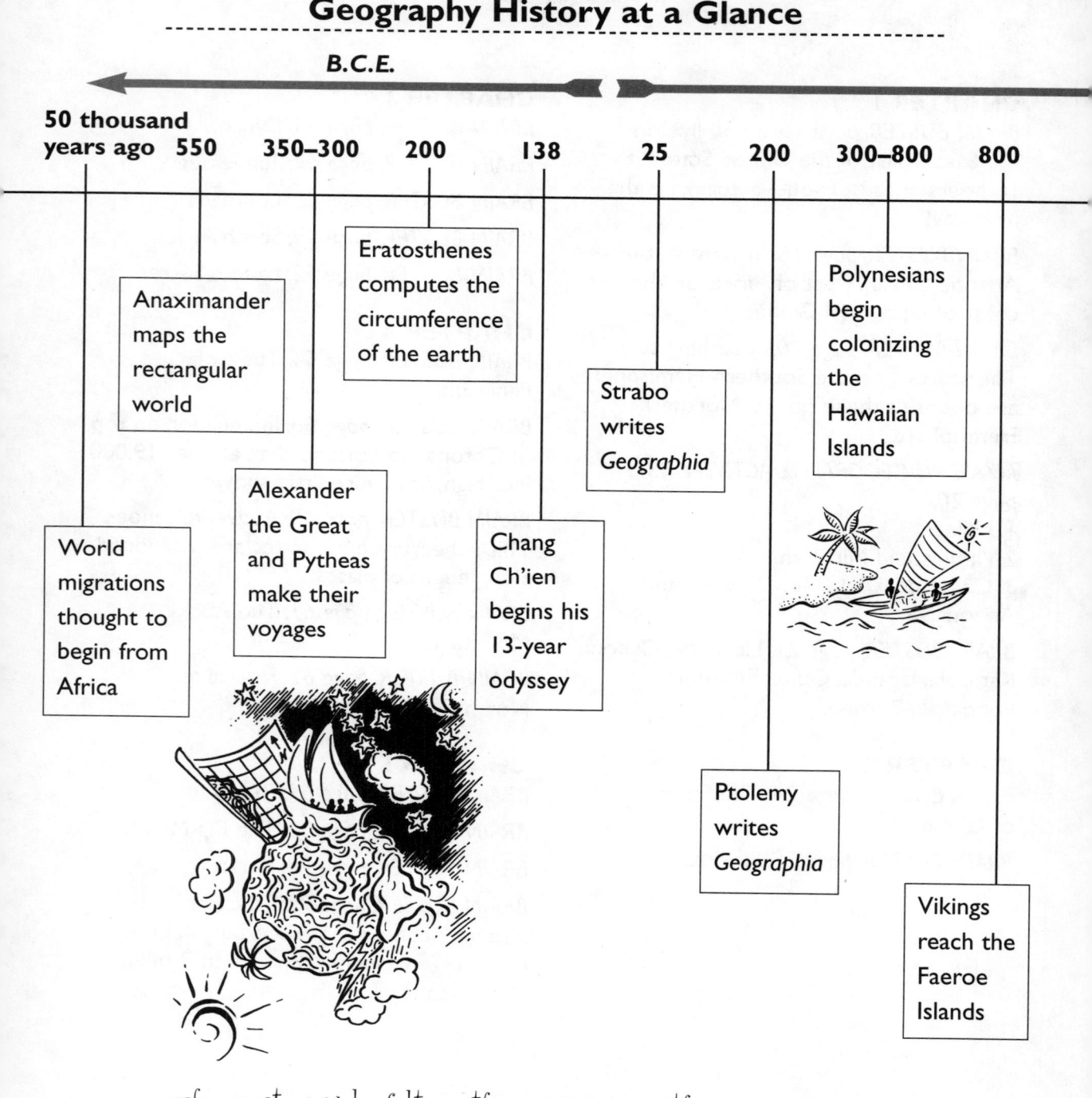

Anaximander maps the rectangular world

Eratosthenes computes the circumference of the earth

Polynesians begin colonizing the Hawaiian Islands

Strabo writes *Geographia*

World migrations thought to begin from Africa

Alexander the Great and Pytheas make their voyages

Chang Ch'ien begins his 13-year odyssey

Ptolemy writes *Geographia*

Vikings reach the Faeroe Islands

The most widely felt earthquakes in North America on record were the New Madrid, Missouri, quakes in 1811–1812—estimated at more than **8.8** magnitude.

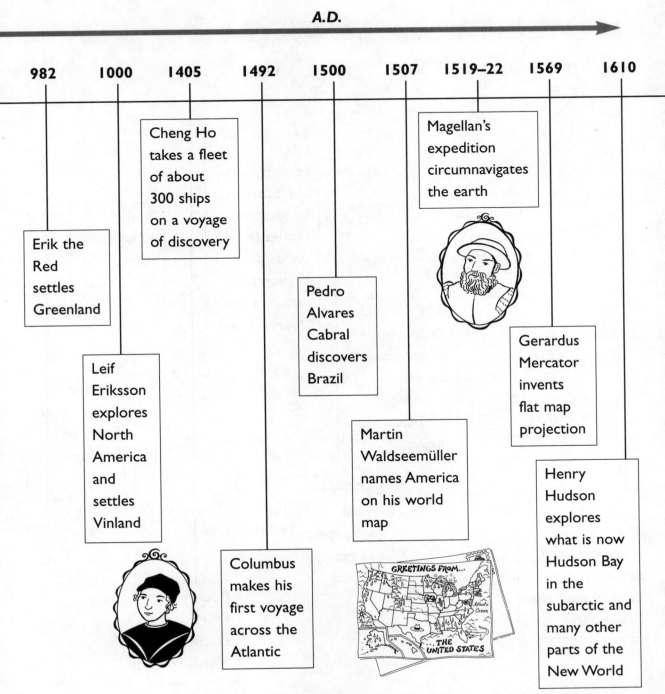

A.D.

| 982 | 1000 | 1405 | 1492 | 1500 | 1507 | 1519–22 | 1569 | 1610 |

Cheng Ho takes a fleet of about 300 ships on a voyage of discovery

Erik the Red settles Greenland

Magellan's expedition circumnavigates the earth

Pedro Alvares Cabral discovers Brazil

Gerardus Mercator invents flat map projection

Leif Eriksson explores North America and settles Vinland

Martin Waldseemüller names America on his world map

Henry Hudson explores what is now Hudson Bay in the subarctic and many other parts of the New World

Columbus makes his first voyage across the Atlantic

GREETINGS FROM...

... THE UNITED STATES

The Eiffel Tower was built in Paris, France, in 18**89**.

A.D.

| 1669 | 1700s | 1784 | 1870 | 1879 | 1890 | 1909 | 1911 | 1912 |

The first map based on triangulation surveying is made, of France

USGS establishes the U.S. Board on Geographic Names (a standardization of geographic names in the United States)

Roald Amundsen reaches the South Pole

H.M.S. *Challenger* completes the first sounding of the ocean depths

Geodesy is introduced

Alfred Wegener announces his theory of Continental Drift

USGS begins formal topographic and geologic mapping

The first scientific world map is drawn on the floor of the Paris Observatory

Robert Peary reaches the North Pole

The world's largest island is Greenland at **90**0,000 square miles.

A.D.

| 1930s | 1957 | 1960 | 1963 | 1964 | 1967 | 1989 | 1990 | 1997 |

Jacques Piccard descends to the Marianas Trench in the *Trieste*

Computer-generated maps are widely used

Alvin, a manned submersible, takes its first dive

The Hubbell space telescope transmits detailed information about the solar system to earth

The first map of the **topography** of the Atlantic Ocean seafloor is created from information gained from echo-sounding devices

Satellites are used for triangulation mapping

El Niño weather systems are widely tracked on the World Wide Web

Photogrammetry is introduced

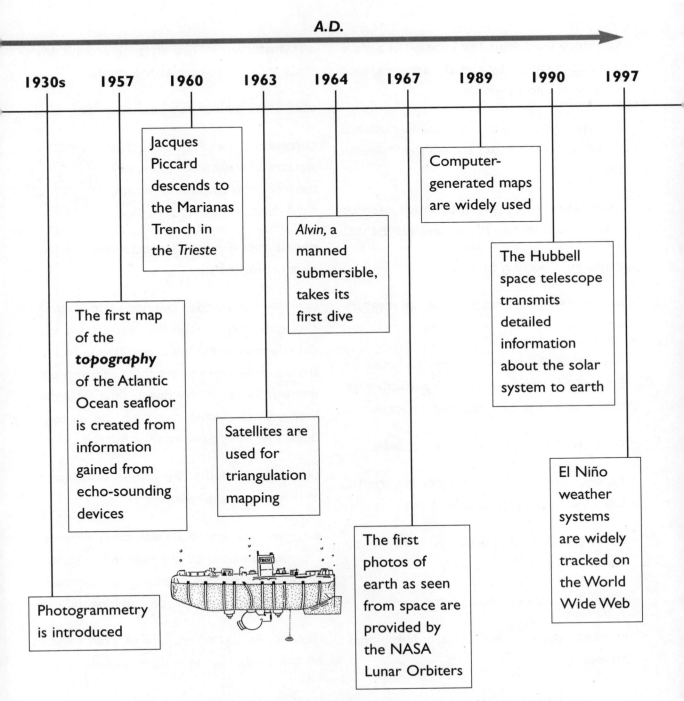

The first photos of earth as seen from space are provided by the NASA Lunar Orbiters

The Panama Canal in Central America was built in 1915.

GLOSSARY

absolute location: The location of a place on earth marked by a grid reference, such as latitude and longitude.

archipelago: A group of islands clustered together in open ocean, such as the Philippine Islands.

astrolabe: An ancient instrument used to measure the position of the stars and the sun.

atlas: A collection of maps.

bar scale: A line on a map used to measure distances.

bematist: A person during the time of Eratosthenes who walked with perfectly even strides as a form of measuring distances.

canyon: A valley with very steep sides.

cape: A point of land that juts out from a coastline; a small cape is called a point or spit.

cartographer: A person who draws or makes maps.

cave: A hollow chamber in the earth.

chronometer: An instrument that measures time.

circumference: The distance around any circle or sphere, such as the earth.

cliff: Steep face of rock, earth, or ice.

compass rose: An object that appears on most maps to identify the four main directions—north, south, east, and west.

continent: A great landmass. The earth has seven continents.

continental divide: The upper ridge along a long mountain range that determines the direction of a continent's river flow. In North and South America, rivers that run down the western slope of the divide flow into the Pacific Ocean, while rivers on the eastern slope eventually flow into the Atlantic.

continental drift: The gradual movement of the seven continents.

degree: The unit of angular measurement. Degrees are used to segment the spherical shape of the earth for geographic purposes, such as measuring latitude and longitude.

desert: An extremely hot or cold region on the earth, with very little rainfall.

Christopher Columbus made his first of four voyages across the Atlantic Ocean in 1492.

elevation: The height of an area above sea level.

epicenter: The area where an earthquake is centered.

equator: The imaginary circle around the widest point of the earth, halfway between the North and South Poles.

fault: A crack or distortion in the earth's crust.

gazetteer: A dictionary of place-names and geographic terms.

geodesy: The study of the size and shape of the earth through applied mathematics.

glacier: A mass of slowly moving ice.

grassland: An open plain covered with grasses.

grid: The pattern of crisscrossing lines on a map that helps pinpoint a particular location.

gulf: A large inlet of ocean partially surrounded by land.

hemisphere: Half of the earth; the half either north or south of the equator or the half either east or west of the prime meridian.

hill: A rounded and elevated area of land, smaller than a mountain.

iceberg: A great mass of ice broken off a glacier.

international date line: The line of longitude that is 180° east and west of the prime meridian; where each calendar day begins.

island: A landmass completely surrounded by water; smaller than a continent.

isthmus (pronounced ISS-muss): A narrow strip of land connecting two larger areas of land.

lake: A large inland body of water.

latitude: Imaginary lines that circle the earth horizontally used to measure how far north or south of the equator a place is located.

lava: Molten rock, or magma, that erupts from a volcano.

legend: The key to the meaning of symbols and pictures on a map.

longitude: Imaginary lines that cross the earth, pole to pole, used to measure distance east or west of the prime meridian.

magma: Molten rock deep beneath the earth's crust.

Crater Lake in Oregon is the deepest lake in the U.S. at 1,932 feet at its deepest point.

mantle: The part of the earth that lies between the core and the crust.

map: A miniature representation of a place, usually on a flat surface.

migration: The movement of people or animals from one place to another.

mountain: A mass of rock high above surrounding land.

ocean ridge: A mountain range along the ocean floor.

ocean trench: A deep, narrow canyon in the ocean floor.

peninsula: An area of land surrounded on three sides by water.

permafrost: Permanently frozen subsoil.

photogrammetry: A photographic technique that gives accurate measurements of the land from photographs taken from the air.

plain: A broad, flat, and nearly treeless land covered with grasses.

plate: A large moving segment of the earth's crust.

plateau: A large highland plain.

plate tectonics: The study of the movement of plates, on which continents and oceans lie.

polar region: A desert with very little precipitation because the air is too cold for clouds to form.

prime meridian: The imaginary line running from the North Pole to the South Pole through Greenwich, England. It is the reference point for longitude and also for time. (Greenwich mean time is the basis for standard time around the world.)

ratio: A comparison. On maps, a ratio is shown on the bar scale.

region: A geographical area distinguished by its physical characteristics and also by the characteristics of the people who live there.

scale: The proportional relationship between a measurement on a map and the actual distance on the surface being measured.

sea level: The level of the ocean surface.

strait: A narrow waterway that connects two larger bodies of water.

surveyor: One who measures and maps the land using a mathematical technique.

In 1947, India won its freedom from Britain.

temperate: A climate without extremes of either heat or cold.

tephra: Solid volcanic material—such as ash, pumice, or rock—ejected during an eruption.

theodolite: A surveying instrument with a telescopic sight for measuring horizontal and vertical angles.

topography: The physical features of a place.

triangulation: A method for surveying, or measuring, distances; it is a way to draw a straight line over the curved surface of the earth.

tropical rain forest: Tropical rain forests occur only in the hot regions close to the equator. They experience heavy rainfall and are rich in both animal and plant life.

tsunami: A huge ocean wave, generated by earth disturbances such as volcanic eruptions or undersea earthquakes.

tundra: The cold, treeless plain above temperate areas.

valley: A gently sloping depression between hills or mountains.

volcano: An opening in a weak spot in the earth's crust where eruptions of molten rock occur.

The highest peak in the continental U.S. is Mt. Whitney, at 14,**495** feet.

INDEX

The greatest recorded age of any scientifically dated rock is 3,**96**3 billion years, found in the N.W. Territory of Canada.